I0002845

It's Not Your Fault!

MILES TYRONE LEADER JR.

outskirtspress
DENVER, COLORADO

Dedication

For those individuals and organizations who have contributed in any manner to my determination to be better than average, and have provided me the fuel to be motivated to achieve the feat of discovering the ultimate investment strategy, I thank you. You, the individuals and organizations that have effectively shaped my perception, and have driven me to not only want to be different from the average person, but also reach my highest potential, I thank you. I am wiser and better for it, and now I can share my knowledge with the world.

This book is dedicated to the prosperity, empowerment, and financial knowledge of all people who seek financial education and economic freedom. We are in a time of great economic change and wealth transfer. I hope enough people can get educated in time to protect themselves from the imminent events on the horizon. Death of ignorance is the only way to become mentally and financially independent. This is a compilation of information I wish was available when I was looking for an opportunity, or financial education.

By design, it is meant for you to be an economic slave. It is not meant for you to have knowledge about the very system that places you into debt and keeps you financially oppressed, nor are you supposed to know the hidden forces that keep you broke as the financial elite get wealthier. This book will educate you and change your perspective about what you think you may know about money, finance, economics and politics. You will also learn secrets to wealth that Wall Street, Bankers and the Government have deliberately kept from you.

It's Not Your Fault!
Written By Miles Tyrone Leader Jr.

Contents

Change Your Perspective

Introduction

People want to believe that the U.S. government acts in the best interest of the citizens. They also want to believe that the Federal Reserve is acting in the best interest of the U.S. economy. The fact of the matter is both of these establishments are acting in a manner that undermines freedom and economic prosperity. The U.S. Government and the Federal Reserve both use deception to fool the citizens into thinking that their policies are to serve and protect the interest of the people. The truth is that their policies only bring about recessions, poverty and bankruptcy. These things will eventually lead to the end of the American way of life that we are all accustomed to living.

Our country's current economic problems stem from our centrally planned monetary system, the individual financial ignorance of people, and the collective ignorance people have of the U.S. Constitution. People make no attempt to understand finance, investing and economics, because they say it's too complicated. The fact is that it's made complicated to keep you ignorant. But, it is actually really simple and easy to understand. Most people don't like being uninformed. However, nothing will ever change until each person takes responsibility for their own actions and starts to change the way they think. You need to change your perspective about money and the current economic conditions, and develop constructive, disciplined actions to better your current situation.

These texts will show you that recessions, poverty and bankruptcies are not only perpetuated by the policies of the Federal Reserve and the U.S. Government, but are also built into the structure of the overall economic design; a design created by groups and forces that want to financially enslave you, and eventually gain control over all governments and economies. If you are living paycheck to paycheck, are always broke or just simply struggling in anyway financially, you need to know, it's not your fault. Understand that your financial failure is built into the system. I will show you how you can change your situation. Forget about the 99 percent - 1 percent propaganda. That is only a device of deception used to distract you from what is really going on in the world; the economic and social division of people, leading to their eventual enslavement, and the control over all the world's resources transferred into the hands of a select group of people.

CHANGE YOUR PERSPECTIVE ❧

Taking Ownership

When people experience failure or poverty, it is often human nature to place the blame for one's situation on the system and a number of other external forces they have absolutely no control over. This helps them to justify their own shortcomings in life. It is also a defensive mechanism that mollifies the guilt a person associates with their failure or poverty, and exonerates their conscience from any feelings of fault. Instead of focusing on the internal forces they do have control over, it's often easier to point the finger, or place the blame elsewhere. An important step in realizing your highest potential financially, or any other way, is to always take ownership over your own successes and failures. Don't justify them.

Taking ownership is only possible if you are proactive in reaching your own goals and achieving success. You must acknowledge and understand that passive, or non-proactive, involvement in your life, career and finances is the main reason for becoming professionally, or financially stagnant. You will never gain anything of value, or prosper from being lackadaisical and freely giving up control over your life. Nobody else is going to push for your prosperity but you.

You must acknowledge and admit to any mistakes you have made personally, professionally, financially and socially and determine the best method to correct those mistakes, if possible. Ask yourself, "What did I do wrong?" and "How can I fix it?" Any person taking ownership over their own successes and failures should be able to find somewhere that they could have been more proactive, if they have thoroughly analyzed their own self and actions.

You must consistently document, or record, yours and

other's research, thoughts, revelations, actions and results of actions. Keep accurate, credible records of important information, meetings and actions for future reference. Conduct yourself with honesty, fairness and integrity at all times in everything you do. By taking ownership over your actions, you will begin to see positive results that would have never come to fruition had you continued living your life placing the blame of your failures on others. Economically and systematically speaking, your situation is not your fault, but you don't have to play the victim either. Take control, and take ownership.

Constructive Actions

Whether we are active, or inactive, our actions fall under two categories, constructive and destructive. You should always strive to ensure that your actions are constructive. The definition of constructive actions would include taking actions that are progressive, or that gradually develop into results. This would also include taking positive steps towards fulfilling a goal, or task. You do this by managing, and being accountable for, your own actions.

Not concerning yourself with the actions of others, unless you are appointed to a supervisory (or leadership) position by a superior (i.e. where your job is to manage others), can also be considered constructive, in the sense of how you have chosen to focus your energy.

Destructive actions don't necessarily refer to destroying, or demolishing something. Destructive actions can be actions that are damaging, in the sense of not being proactive. Someone who is not proactive in their personal, professional, financial or social affairs, are exhibiting destructive actions by doing nothing. Since doing nothing is doing something, hence the word doing, it indicates the action of not taking action, being passive or non-participant. This is basically leaving your fate to chance, or in the hands of others. Since no one will ensure your financial independence and success but you, you cannot be passive in your personal, professional, financial and social affairs.

SWOT Analysis

An individual or business's potential for success in any venture pursued can be determined by both Internal Forces and External Forces. Both of these forces can be broken into two categories, Internal "Strengths and Weaknesses", and External "Opportunities and Threats". Analysis of an individual, or business, in this manner is referred to as the S.W.O.T. Analysis. The S.W.O.T. (alternately referred to as S.L.O.T.) Analysis is a strategic planning method, which evaluates the Strengths, Weaknesses (or Limitations), Opportunities and Threats of a project or business venture. This can also be applied to any individual person.

In relation to changing your perspective, a person should only concern themselves with their internal forces, maximizing their strengths and minimizing their weaknesses. A person should not concern themselves with the external forces of opportunities and threats, because they have absolutely no control over these forces. By maximizing your strengths and minimizing your weaknesses, you will set yourself up to take advantage of opportunities when they present themselves, and avert or minimize any threats that may arise.

When conducting a S.W.O.T. Analysis, you must focus on and list the following:

Internal (Controllable) Forces: What you have control over and where you should focus most of your time and energy.

Strengths: Anything that provides the subject an advantage. Anything the subject is extraordinary at, or efficient in doing. The subject should always focus on increasing its strengths to become better.

Weaknesses (Limitations): Anything that places the subject at a disadvantage. Anything the subject must improve or correct. A deficiency. The subject should always focus on minimizing its weaknesses to become less vulnerable.

External (Uncontrollable) Forces: What you do not have control over and where you should not focus a great deal of time and energy.

Opportunities: Anything that can greatly improve, enhance or increase potential for success. The subject should position itself to take advantage of potential opportunities that may occur by maximizing its strengths and minimizing its weaknesses.

Threats: Anything that can potentially hinder, harm or damage potential for success. The subject should always hedge against potential threats to avoid destructive effects of a collapse, disaster or catastrophe by having some form of insurance.

Internal Forces	External Forces
Strengths What You Are Really Good At.	**Opportunities** What Can Potentially Help You.
Weaknesses What You Are Not Really Good At.	**Threats** What Can Potentially Hurt You.

Note: This is the simplest example of internal and external forces affecting a person or business.

Learn Money Management

Assets vs. Liabilities

Before you can begin establishing your financial independence, you must understand something very basic; the difference between assets and liabilities. Most people consider anything they own, or something they spent a lot of money on, as being an asset. Understand that most personal possessions depreciate in value, so they are not worth the same amount of money as when you bought them. You may like to consider things like your house, car and high definition television as assets, but the honest truth is they are not assets. Regardless of your perception of what an asset or liability is, you must understand and retain these basic concepts:

1. An asset is anything of value that generates a positive income for the owner, whether through passive investing, capital gains or some form of recurring income.
2. A liability is anything, or anyone, that costs money to utilize, or maintain them, and/ or does not generate a positive income for the owner or user.

Net Worth

> This is what you are worth
>
> Your Total $ Value

Assets

> Generate a positive income
>
> Add to net worth

Liabilities

> Cost Money
>
> Lower net worth

Owner's Equity

> Net Worth
>
> Total Asset & Liabilities

Balance Sheet

Most people don't usually record their income and expenses on a spreadsheet or ledger. Only when they decide to make a big purchase (e.g. a 50 inch high definition TV or a home entertainment center) do they even look to see if they have cash in their account to cover the purchase, or monthly payments. People don't usually know off the top of their head how much cash, fixed expenses and debt they have, or what their net worth is. If they actually took the time to lay their finances out on a visual platform, they would probably see that they have a negative net worth. It's a scary sight; a big, red or negative number.

How does one determine their net worth? It is one of the simplest tools of accounting; The Balance Sheet. This lists all of your assets (i.e. equipment, investments and cash on hand) and all of your liabilities (i.e. long term debt, accounts payable, short term debt) to determine your owner's equity (net worth).

Here is an example:

Balance Sheet - 2013	
Assets	
Cash and Cash Equivalents	$100,000
Inventory / Equipment / Property	$300,000
Receivables	$29,000
Total Assets	**$429,000**
Liabilities	
Short Term Debt	$4,000
Accounts Payable	$11,000
Long Term Debt	$270,000
Other Current Debt	$3,000
Total Liabilities	**288,000**
Owner's Equity	**$141,000**

Cashflow & Income Statement

A cashflow statement is a report detailing the flow, or movement, of cash (cash in and cash out) from operations, investments and financing, and the increase or decrease in cash. An income statement is a report detailing your gross revenue (income), total expenses, income after expenses then income after interest and taxes.

By tracking both your cashflow (i.e. income after expenses) and your net income (i.e. earnings after taxes), you can see how much money you have coming in from work, investments or business and how much disposable income you have left. This will help you understand where cash is going to, and how efficient you are at household, or business, money management, and capital allocation. This can provide valuable insight into how profitable, well managed or valuable an enterprise is.

Income Statement – 2013	
Revenue	
Total Revenue	$50,000
Cost of Revenue	($10,000)
Gross Profits	**$40,000**
Operating Expenses	
Research Development	$13,000
Selling / Administrative	$5,000
Non-Recurring	$7,000
Other	$11,000
Total Operating Expenses	**$36,000**
Operating Income	**$4,000**
Income Tax	**$1,000**
Income After Tax	**$3,000**
Net Income	**$3,000**

Cashflow Statement – 2013	
Net Income	**$3,000**
Cash from (used by) Operations	
Depreciation	($100)
Change in Accts. Rec.	$450
Change in Operations	$450
Total Cash from Operations	**$800**
Cash from (used by) Investments	
Capital Expenditures	($10,000)
Investments	$5,000
Other Cash from Investments	$6,000
Total Cash from (used by) Investments	**$1,000**
Cash from (used by) Financing	
Distributions/ Dividends	($2,000)
Sale of Units/ Stock/ Equity	$2,000
Net Borrowing	$20,000
Other Cash from Financing	($10,000)
Total Cash from (used by) Financing	**$10,000**
Change in Cashflow	**$8,800**

As you can see from the visual depictions below, assets bring cash in, and liabilities create expenses and take cash out. The arrows represent cashflow:

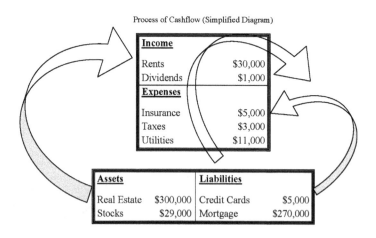

Process of Cashflow (Simplified Diagram)

Forecasting

Either by using a spreadsheet, a cashflow app or creating a hand written list, you can predict how much cash after expenses you will have in the future (e.g. one month, 6 months, 1 year), or how much disposable income you will have for recreation, or investing, at a predetermined time, based on your current income and fixed expenses. This is called forecasting. This is probably one of the most responsible ways to track your income and expenses. This will ensure:

- You don't spend what you don't have.
- You don't miss any payment due dates.
- You will be able to allot money for other things (e.g. recreation, investing)
- You have a broad view and detailed knowledge of your financial state, and your net worth.

If you forecast your income and expenses using a cashflow app, spreadsheet or some type of computerized calculator program, you can always adjust amounts later to compensate for changes in income, expenses or allotments. This money management technique makes you completely aware of your finances, and gives you the power of fairly accurate financial projections. See our example.

SIMPLE INCOME & EXPENSES FORECAST

Cable (2/20/20xx)	($100) – Payment	$2,900
Car Note (2/19/20xx)	($200) – Payment	$3,000
Paycheck (2/12/20xx)	$1,000 - Direct Deposit	$3,200
Rent (2/5/20xx)	($300) – Payment	$2,200
Paycheck (1/29/20xx)	$1,000 - Direct Deposit	$2,500
Water (1/25/20xx)	($100) - Payment	$1,500
Electricity (1/25/20xx)	($100) - Payment	$1,600
Gas (1/25/20xx)	($100) - Payment	$1,700
Auto Insurance (1/21/20xx)	($100) - Payment	$1,800
Cable (1/20/20xx)	($100) - Payment	$1,900
Car Note (1/19/20xx)	($200) - Payment	$2,000
Paycheck (1/15/20xx)	$1,000 - Direct Deposit	$2,200
Rent (1/5/20xx)	($300) - Payment	$1,200
Paycheck (1/1/20xx)	$1,000 - Direct Deposit	$1,500

Reducing Your Debt

On a note (debt instrument), or loan, paying any amount over your monthly minimum balance due (even by $0.01) can significantly reduce your principal balance over time. Remember this, banks add interest (the cost of borrowing) to your principal balance (the amount you borrowed) and calculate your payments based on an amortized schedule of principal and interest payments you must make over time. Banks, lenders and other financial institutions are maximizing their profits at your expense and financial detriment.

You can put a monkey wrench into their calculations by over paying on the monthly balance. Free up your cash faster. And, never pay the minimum balance. Paying the minimum balance mostly goes to pay the interest (i.e. bank profits) payments to the bank and takes you more time, and cash, to pay off the loan over the long run.

Remember, financial institutions like banks, insurance companies and brokers do not have your best interest in mind. They operate in their own financial interest. They all assess the safest, most profitable way to get money out of you and keep you as a paying client. Stop paying, or terminate your affiliation with them and they will not help you. They will never educate you on how to maximize your own wealth unless it is to benefit their own agenda; which it probably won't.

Hedge, Don't Save

People who save their money are financially losers. How, do you ask? In 1971, the U.S. Dollar stopped being a store of value, or what we all like to refer to as money, and effectively the U.S. Dollar became a currency (no longer a store of value). This was the year the dollar was taken off the "Gold Standard" by then President Richard Nixon when he terminated the dollar's convertibility into gold and silver under the Bretton-Wood System. The U.S. Dollar was no longer backed by gold. So basically, the U.S. Government could borrow as much cash as it needed to spend from the Federal Reserve, who could now freely create as much cash as it wanted, opening the floodgates to inflation.

This is comparable to giving a prescription drug addict the keys to a pharmacy. The Federal Reserve creates currency (out of thin air) recklessly and irresponsibly. The more currency created the more each dollar's value declines. When money is changed to a currency and the central bank can freely create as much cash as it wants, this eventually causes the currency's decline towards its true value of zero. So, if you are saving, you are losing money. Your purchasing power is steadily declining.

A smart way to protect your hard earned wealth from the steady decline in purchasing power is for you to invest your cash into assets (income producing properties), and hedge against potential loss. You should hedge against potential losses by placing safety mechanisms (e.g. insurance, puts and stop- losses) in order to protect yourself.

The ways to hedge against loss are to:

- Don't be ignorant and stubborn to financial education.
- Understand that the dollar is declining in value.
- Understand inflation decreases the purchasing power of currency.
- Don't Save, Invest.
- Purchase income-producing properties (assets).
- Place safety mechanisms in order to protect yourself (or hedge) against losses.

At the rate that the dollar is declining, even if you are lucky enough to get 1 to 2 percent interest from the banks, your gains still cannot keep up with your losses. Inflation negates any gains you may receive at 1 to 2 percent.

As value of the dollar declines and taxes increase, prices increase as well.

The ones who foot the bill are the middle class taxpayers. *"Regardless of what any politician promises you in order to keep their position of power, the middle class will always foot the bill for tax and price increases, because the consumer gets the cost passed on to them"*.

Certain key events have been the main factors in the decline and destruction of the dollar.

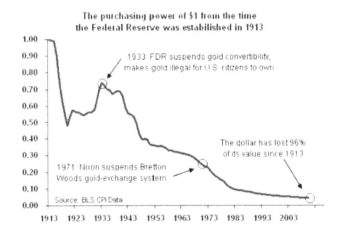

The purchasing power of $1 from the time the Federal Reserve was established in 1913

1933 FDR suspends gold convertibility, makes gold illegal for U.S. citizens to own

The dollar has lost 96% of its value since 1913

1971 Nixon suspends Bretton Woods gold-exchange system

Source: BLS CPI Data

Establish Financial Knowledge

Three Types of Education

One of the first steps to financial education is to understand that *there are three types of education: academic, professional* and *financial*. **Academic education** provides you the Adult Basic Education (ABE) of **reading**, **writing** and **arithmetic**. This education occurs from grades K through 12, and provides you the most basic knowledge and communication skills.

Academic Education

Reading ABC, XYZ / Cat, Hat / Dog, Log	Writing My Signature	Arithmetic 1+1=2 / 2x2=4 / 5x+5=30

Professional education is your academic career at a college or university, in preparation for a paid career. This is where you learn basic business skills, or a specialized trade, to become a productive, self managing employee for a company.

Professional Education

M.B.A. / M.S. / M.S.W. Career in Business or Administration Fields	Ph.D. / D.D.S. / J.D. Career in Medicine, Law or other Professional Fields	B.A / B.S / B.B.A / Certified Basic Educational Requirement for Most Careers

And last, **financial education** is the education not taught in high school or college. This is the education that separates the millionaire businessperson who lives in a mansion, drives a Bentley, and travels around the world from the office worker who rents an apartment, takes the bus and has to request a day off months in advance. This is the same education that separates the billionaire investor from the struggling store manager. Financial education prepares you to be a big business owner or an investor who is in control of their time and income.

Financial Education

Money Currency, Monetary System, Inflation, Debt, Types of Cashflow	Investing Economics, Asset Classes, Generating Cashflow, Return on Investment, Compounding Returns, Exit Strategies	Finance Financial Statements, Accounting, Credit Management, Risk Hedging

It's no mistake that financial education is not taught in high schools or colleges. You are provided an education preparing you to become a worker (i.e. servant) providing a service in exchange for a wage. You are not taught to become a business owner or investor.

Give a person a fish, they eat for a day. Teach a person to fish, they eat for the rest of their life... This is our company's mindset. Building a dependency on handouts creates further dependency. Becoming self-sufficient creates independence. The financial elite do not want the middle class or the poor to get a financial education, because it breaks the economic control they have over dependent, financially uneducated people.

Types of Income and Earners

You should understand how income is earned, but first you must understand the types of income. Even though people fall under one of the four types of income earners, there are three types of income. They are as follows:

Earned Income – Any income that is earned based on your

personal time and effort (e.g. wages, salaries, commissions or tips) is considered earned income. This income involves your labor or your services. If you don't work, you don't get paid.

Portfolio Income – Any income that is earned from the sale of an investment that has appreciated in value is considered portfolio income. This includes proceeds from any investment sold such as paper assets (e.g. stocks or bonds), real estate or other assets that provide income from appreciation or "Capital Gains".

Passive Income – Any income that is earned from the purchase or creation of an asset is considered passive income. This includes big business owners who use the leverage of a system or labor, real estate investors who lease their property to tenants and owners of intellectual property (copyrights, patents and trademarks) who receive royalties and licensing fees. Passive income means you create the asset, acquire or build the asset and it continues to generate income independent of the owner's time and effort.

When it pertains to how income is earned, people fall under one of four categories; employees, self-employed (small business), business owners and investors. No one particular category is better than another, but understanding the fundamentals of earning income for each category will help you understand how the poor get poorer, the rich get richer and the wealthy stay wealthy.

Employees work for a person or entity and trade their time for money; either an hourly wage, a set salary or commission (i.e. performance based pay). Most employees will never be rich because their income is limited by the amount of hours they work and the amount they are compensated. Relating to income taxation, they earn their money, get taxed first then spend what's left.

Self-employed (e.g. small business owners, dentists, lawyers, contractors) are professionals trained in a specialty, or other small business owners. Their income is limited by the amount of hours they work. Relating to income taxation, they earn their income, pay for expenses first and then get taxed on the remaining revenue.

Business Owners are people who own a system or a business, which usually does not require them to be present to earn income. They employ people and/ or an automated system to operate their business and pay set wages for time and labor. The business earns income, pays for expenses first and then gets taxed on the remaining revenue (cashflow or net operating income). The business owner can receive a distribution or dividend from the profits.

Investors are the opposite of employees. Instead of trading their time for money, they trade their money for time. In other words, their money works for them by receiving a fixed or variable return on an investment in addition to the original amount invested. They make money either through distributions, dividends or when the investment is sold for a profit (capital gain). Investors earn money and are taxed on the realized gains (i.e. actual profits received), and usually at a favorable tax rate (unlike employee income), sometimes with more deductions, than employees. Note: Investors can multiply their income by reinvesting profits.

Employee – earned income (Self)	Business Owner – passive income (System)
You Work Get Taxed - Get Paid + Take Home + Pay Expenses –	**System Works** Get Paid + Pay Expenses – Get Taxed – Distribute Profits (or Reinvest) +
Self Employed – earned income (Self)	Investor – portfolio/ passive income (Money)
You Work Get Paid + Pay Expenses - Get Taxed - Take Home +	**Money Works** Get Paid + Get Taxed - Take Home + Pay Expenses -

As taught by investor and entrepreneur Robert T. Kiyosaki.

Programmed to be Broke

Have you ever noticed how we, as a society, are programmed to be broke? We are trained to be in debt, spend beyond our means, and utilize credit, which is an I.O.U. (i.e. I owe you, more than I borrowed), to finance liabilities. This is an intentional psychological programming created by an elaborate hierarchy that intends to keep us as economic (wage) slaves, indentured servants and labor resources working tirelessly to make the banks and big corporations richer. These intentional psychological programs and blatant lies include:

How we are being encouraged to finance huge liabilities (e.g. automobiles and houses) by using credit. We are conditioned to think that we have to apply for a loan, which will take anywhere from 15 up to 30 years to pay off, to make large purchases, while incurring huge interest costs. We are conditioned to think that paying off debt over a long period of time is good. The truth is it costs you more money the longer it takes to pay off a loan.

How we are being programmed to think that the only method of purchasing a car or house is by going through a bank. The fact of the matter is, there is at least one incredible and highly beneficial alternative to finance a large purchase without going through a bank. I will cover that option later.

How we are being deceived into believing that without good personal credit, you can never finance real estate or an automobile. For one, personal credit is more dangerous than helpful... and two, you could have the worst credit in the world and still finance real estate, automobiles or even a business. You just have to know what to do, and then have the discipline to properly implement it.

How we are being deceived into believing that a FICO score is the most important tool in financial independence. Honestly, a FICO score is okay. But there are other measures of your credit worthiness such as a DUNS number or even better, an income statement and balance sheet. If you have those looking perfect, no credit score can ever trump that.

Personal Credit

Personal credit is not an asset. Remember, assets are anything or anyone that generates a positive income for the owner or user. Credit is a means of financing a purchase without having all the funds upfront. With credit, you pay more back to the lender with interest than you actually borrowed as the principle. So, it costs you money to utilize credit. The only way credit becomes an asset is if you are using the credit to purchase an investment that will bring you a positive income after all expenses are paid and debts are serviced. Otherwise, credit is a liability and nothing more; despite what people may say. Remember, personal credit should only be used to purchase investments.

If you plan to purchase a house to live in, buying a duplex, triplex or quadruplex may be the best choice, if you are financing (borrowing the funds). You can live in the property and rent out the remaining unit(s). You can have a real home-based business and receive a passive monthly income from your home. Living in a single family home doesn't allow you to rent out the property. Remember, your credit is only an asset when the property financed is generating you (the owner) a positive income, with no extra money coming out of your pocket.

Meaning of Investment
A lot of times, people use the word "investment" in the same connotation as purchasing something they need, or simply want. They will refer to the purchase of a new house, a new car, a new bed, or even a new television as investing in those items. While they may be great purchases for their intended purposes, they are not investments. An investment (financially speaking) is the act or process of acquiring something (or any person's services) for the specific purpose of producing a profit or passive income.

The misuse and misunderstanding of the word "investment" by middle class and poor citizens destructively enables them to squander money on depreciating objects. Remember these simple points: 1. Buying a house can be considered an investment, if you plan to sell the property in the near future for a profit, or rent out any extra units for a passive income, 2. Buying a car, a television and other depreciating items is not an investment. You are purchasing a liability, 3. An investment is the action or process of acquiring an asset, 4. Assets are tangible, and intangible, property, owned or used by a person or entity, which generate a positive income for the owner or user.

The Monetary System

The Monetary System is the way in which our money comes into existence. Only the most savvy and ambitious people take the time to truly understand our monetary system. There are two types of monetary systems; commodity and fiat. A commodity money system is one where a commodity like gold is the unit of value and used as money. A fiat money system is where currency, or paper notes, are issued by a central bank and made legal tender by government decree (fiat) or law.

In a fiat monetary system, money (currency) can be exponentially inflated to meet government's desired level of spending. A commodity based, or commodity backed, money system is considered a sound money system, because it cannot be exponentially increased by the central bank. America, and most of the developed world, currently operates under a fiat money system. Various financial opportunities and threats arise based on decisions being made in our current monetary system. If understood, this system can create millionaires out of regular people.

We work within this system, and make our livelihoods through this system. This system controls both our income, and our debt. This system controls our economic prosperity, and our recession into poverty. The impact this system has on our everyday lives is so profound, that the average poor and middle class American cannot fathom the magnitude, or complexity of it. We have accepted this system for what it is, due to our lack of financial education in primary school, undergraduate school, graduate school, and due to how our parents raised us to understand and perceive money.

Money is Debt

To understand the dynamics of our economy and financial system, you must know and understand one thing about what we refer to as money; and that is money is debt. What we all know to be money (i.e. the cash in our pockets) is not money, but is in fact what is called a currency. This currency comes into existence in two ways. About 3 percent is actually physically printed up by the Federal Reserve via the U.S. Treasury and circulated into the economy as "Base Money", which we can hold in our hands and spend. The other 97 percent is borrowed into existence, or created out of thin air, through loans provided by our Financial System to the U.S. Government, businesses and the public. So, in order for 97 percent of our currency to exist, it must first be borrowed into existence by the government, businesses and subsequently through consumer loans. This happens through the debt based monetary system of a private Central Bank.

The Federal Reserve is the Central Bank of the United States. The Federal Reserve controls the supply of U.S. currency and interest rates to borrow that currency. As the Central Bank, they have virtually absolute power to set the monetary policy of our country.

Because of the economic propaganda we have been fed by our government and the international bankers who created, own and control the Federal Reserve, we look at currency as something of value. Although, at one point in history this was true (i.e. when our currency was under the Bretton-Wood System), in today's economy, it's a false statement. Our money is fiat currency, sanctioned as legal tender by the government for all debts, public and private. And, every dollar you hold in your pocket represents debt, not value.

Money vs. Currency

The distinction between money and currency is vague. If you don't know what to look for, or what the economic conditions are, you would never know if the cash in your pocket is in fact a currency, or money. The cash we hold in the bank and conduct transactions with is in fact a currency. Here is how one can determine if the cash they hold is a currency. Both money and currency have the following characteristics: Portable, Divisible, Fungible and Durable. But, where money is a store of value ---meaning your purchasing power doesn't decline over time through inflation--- currency is simply a claim check on value. Money occurs naturally, like gold and silver, where currency is artificial and can be printed exponentially (or created out of thin air) until it declines to its true value of zero. Money is true value where currency loses value through inflation, and carries debt.

Every unit of currency created out of thin air, or physically printed up, and circulated into the economy steals value from existing currency in circulation. Our currency is fiat and backed by nothing but the full faith and credit of the United States, and the faith people have in it to be able to purchase goods and services. Decreasing the value of the currency through inflation is like a hidden tax on the middle class, savers and anyone else who doesn't understand the nature of our monetary system. This tax benefits those who create the money or get to use it first in the economy. Once it gets to the wage slave and is deposited into the bank, it has lost a significant portion of its value due to inflation.

When people think about wealth, they think of paper currency; or what we all consider to be money. The mindset is, the more paper currency you have in your bank account, the more wealth you have. But, wealth is not determined by the amount of Dollars, Euros or any other paper currency you may have in a bank account, vault, briefcase, or under a mattress. All currencies are made legal tender simply by government decree (fiat) and are issued as the accepted medium of exchange in which we can conduct transactions to buy and sell goods and services. By no means is currency the real wealth.

Currencies are all given value by government decree and can be exponentially created out of thin air by the central bank. In essence, $100 today may only be worth $98, or less, next year (at 2 percent inflation) because the currency can be inflated at will. It takes more currency in the future to purchase the same amount of goods and services that you can buy today.

All currencies are debt with interest attached to them, and the supply must be perpetually expanded or the financial system will collapse. The currency you consider to be wealth actually loses value every year. In fact, it is a debt owed to the private Central Bank. So, every dollar, euro, pound etc. you hold is debt, and not wealth. A currency note is simply a claim check on real value; an obligation of the receiver to pay a debt that is mathematically designed to be defaulted on.

Understand that for 5,000 years, the only true forms of money have been gold and silver. These are naturally occurring commodities, which cannot be created out of thin air, or artificially inflated. Plus, there is no debt attached to gold and silver, and our U.S. Constitution (the law of the land) states that only gold and silver are legal tender, not artificially created fiat currency.

Real Money - Natural Represents Value	Claim Check – Artificial Note / Represents Debt

Money Creation (IOU for an IOU)

The Federal Reserve, which is the entity that controls our debt-based monetary system, and the supply of our country's fiat currency, lends our national currency to our government at interest, automatically putting our government into debt. This basically occurs when the government issues a debt instrument called a treasury bond (i.e. an IOU) to the Federal Reserve in exchange for Federal Reserve Notes (another IOU, with no actual money or reserves backing it). From this transaction, U.S. Legal Tender, or U.S. Dollars, spring into existence. This currency then gets spent into the economy for government obligations, operations and programs.

After this transaction takes place, the government now owes a debt to the Federal Reserve, but with interest attached to it. One question that should arise from this is, "Where does the money come from to pay for the interest?" The answer is, "Nowhere". That money doesn't exist. So the debt our government incurs can never actually be paid back, because the interest owed on the loan is in excess of the principal amount in circulation. Every dollar in circulation represents debt owed back to the Federal Reserve, plus a percentage of interest.

For us as Americans to enjoy our current prosperity as a country, the government has to borrow from the future. What does this mean and how can the government borrow from the future? Well, simply put, we are being taxed now for the debts incurred by government years ago. And, we will continue to be taxed in the future for debts incurred today. We work 3 months (or more) out of the year to pay taxes to our government. That cash goes directly into the pockets of the Federal Reserve's shareholders (Yes, shareholders like a corporation).

The Federal Reserve is a publicly chartered privately owned corporation. We as taxpayers are indentured servants to the Federal Reserve, working tirelessly to pay the interest on a debt we didn't personally incur. The government taxes us to pay the Federal Reserve interest on cash created and lent out by the Federal Reserve. The Federal Reserve pays its shareholders a 6% annual dividend by law from these payments. Most people are none the wiser due to the ignorance they have about our financial and monetary systems.

Fractional Reserve Banking

Banks are required by the Federal Reserve to have approximately only 10 percent (now it's probably less) reserves on hand to satisfy any depositor demands. A depositor demand is the cash you or I would withdraw from the bank for our everyday transactions and cash purchases. This means that if there is $1,000,000 in deposits, the bank legally only has to have $100,000 on hand to back the deposits of $1,000,000. Any excess over that amount (let's say $900,000) can be used for investments, or to make loans to the public. But, loans made to the public do not come out of the excess of reserves. That excess, never actually transfers to the borrower.

So, how does the bank make loans, you ask? Out of thin air! When a person goes to a bank to get a loan, the cash for that loan comes from the signature of the borrower. By signing a promissory note, the borrower is making a promise to repay a loan they'll never actually receive. Their signature has created the cash for the loan. The bank simply types bank credits (i.e. currency) into the borrower's account, or does a basic check book entry reflecting this new loan. The bank also types bank credits into the account holder's account to hide the fact that 90 percent of their deposits have been stolen, as the currency is deposited into the account of a seller. This ten percent requirement and expansion of the currency supply is called the "Fractional Reserve System".

The borrower is now obligated to repay the loan they signed for, with interest. And worst of all, they are usually required to put up some form of property as collateral. In the event they are unable to repay this loan, the bank will take their property. All because of the fractional reserve system and the request for a loan, what you think is money has now been created out of nothing. And, debt was created from lending money that didn't actually exist.

Every time a deposit is made into a bank, these same Fractional Reserve System rules apply. Whether currency is credited to an account, a direct deposit or an ATM deposit is made, they can repeat this trick with any cash entered as new deposits. They can create up to ten times the amount of money for each deposit made. Ten thousand dollars can be multiplied into $100,000 without ever actually lending a physical dollar. The banks can do this even if they make the loan and the currency is deposited back with that same bank.

Account Holder Deposits $10,000	Banks Reserve Requirement $1,000	Excess Bank Can Lend from Accounts $9,000
Cash from loans are created Upon signature of borrower	Remaining Account Deposits $1,000	*Account holder cash is credited to account of a seller*

Because of our perceived value of money, we equate making money, or "getting money" as increasing our monetary value. This is wrong. When you say, "I'm getting money", you are actually saying, "I'm getting debt", because money (i.e. our currency) represents debt. We need to start saying, "I'm building wealth" and actually build wealth. How do we build wealth? You build wealth by using currency to acquire assets (i.e. income producing properties) and make investments. Currency is a medium in which to acquire wealth. Currency isn't the wealth. Think of currency like points you accumulate towards the real prize. Real wealth (the prize) comes in the form of natural resources and commodities.

For anyone who believes that hoarding (or saving) our fiat currency is building wealth, they are sadly mistaken, and mislead. Our currency was taken off of the (Bretton-Wood) gold standard in 1971. This was the check system that limited the amount of currency our government could borrow and the Federal Reserve could create and circulate into the economy.

The more currency circulated into the economy, disproportionate to the production of goods and services, the less value it has. Increased money supply without increased production, devalues all currency in circulation. Our currency is not backed by gold, or anything for that matter. What keeps it functional as a currency is the faith people have that they can purchase what they need, and conveniently conduct transactions with it. Currency is simply a medium of exchange, which is accepted as payment for goods and services.

Fractional Reserve Banking affects the middle class, because it steals wealth and purchasing power from the depositors who save their currency in the bank, and transfers that wealth to the banks. Banks dilute the value of each dollar in the depositors' bank accounts through loans provided with currency that doesn't even exist. It also creates economic slavery through theft of wealth and legalized counterfeiting of a currency. Banks can inflate the currency supply at will through loans and credit cards. We must sell our time and labor to earn wages denominated in currency, only to have that currency inflated and devalued by the banks, and our wages taxed by government.

The Federal Reserve, the Treasury and Congress

The U.S. Federal Reserve Bank is the Central Bank of the United States of America. The Federal Reserve is charged with conducting our nation's monetary policy (i.e. controlling the money supply and interest rates). The Federal Reserve is also responsible for supervising & regulating banks, maintaining stability of our financial system and providing financial services to depository institutions, the U.S. Government and foreign official institutions. Although they are required to turn over any excess cash to the U.S. Treasury after operating expenses and shareholder dividends are paid, the Federal Reserve is completely independent of government, doesn't have to submit to any audit and has virtually complete control over our economy through control of credit and currency.

Two mandates given to the Federal Reserve by Congress when the Federal Reserve Act of 1913 was passed were maximum employment and stable prices. This was called the Federal Reserve "Duel Mandate". Time has shown that the Federal Reserve has not lived up to these mandates.

The U.S. Treasury (under the Executive Branch of government) is charged with managing our government's revenue. The Treasury's responsibilities include printing all paper currency and minting all coins through the Bureau of Engraving and Printing, Collecting all federal taxes through the Internal Revenue Service, and Managing U.S. government debt instruments, except those held by the Federal Reserve. The Federal Reserve manages its own U.S. government bonds.

U.S. Congress (comprised of The Senate and The House of Representatives) is the legislative branch of government. They have the power to enact laws, authorize taxation of citizens and control government spending and declaration of war.

Along with the Judicial Branch, which is responsible for interpreting laws enacted by congress, there are only 3 Branches of government. However, the Federal Reserve acts like an unofficial 4th branch. The Federal Reserve controls the blood of our economy, while operating outside of the checks and balances system. They are not bound by the rules of the checks and balances system of our government. When the Federal Reserve was established on December 23, 1913, our government began to borrow its own money with interest from the Federal Reserve; a private entity, controlled by international bankers. The government distributes the currency it borrows into the various government agencies, programs and to government contractors. To fund its operations and pay its obligations, the government must continue to borrow money, at interest, from the Federal Reserve.

Learn Basic Economics

Economics

Economics is the social science that analyzes the production, distribution, and consumption of goods and services. If you know the two main categories of economics and have knowledge of the factors that affect each one, you can gain a better understanding of various financial opportunities that are available in different economic situations. The two main categories of economics are Microeconomics and Macroeconomics.

Microeconomics: This examines the behavior of basic elements in the economy, including individual markets* and agents (such as consumers and firms, buyers and sellers). A particular market (e.g. real estate market, stock market, job market) may be affected by various factors such as perception, economic booms or busts, construction and a variety of other things. What is happening on a national macro level may not be happening on a local micro level in some areas. That is why in bad economies savvy investors who know tricks of the market can make a lot of cash while regular people suffer through the recessions. *Market: A regular gathering of people for the purchase and sale of provisions, livestock, and other commodities.

Macroeconomics: This addresses issues affecting an entire economy, including unemployment, inflation, economic growth, monetary policy and fiscal policy.

- **Unemployment:** The number or proportion of people who are unemployed. This number only factors in the people who are claiming unemployment benefits and not those who are underemployed or stopped claiming benefits all together. The official government unemployment statistics may state one rate of unemployment, but the actual unemployment rate may be significantly higher.
- **Inflation**: The general increase in prices and fall in the purchasing power, or value, of money. When prices increase that is called Price Inflation. However, monetary Inflation is when the supply of money (i.e. currency) is increased significantly or exponentially. Prices will eventually rise due to the increase of currency units chasing finite goods, services and commodities.

- **Economic Growth**: The increasing capacity of the economy to satisfy the wants of the members of society. When people's consumption increases due to increased demand, or increased supply, and the economy can continue to meet their consumption demand, that's what would be considered economic growth.
- **Monetary Policy**: The process by which the monetary authority (i.e. a central bank) of a country controls the supply of money (i.e. currency), often targeting a rate of interest for the purpose of promoting economic growth and stability.
- **Fiscal Policy**: A government policy for dealing with the budget (especially with taxation and borrowing). A government's fiscal policy is basically determining how much money the government can spend and how much it can borrow in order to run a deficit and meet its spending needs. In a fiat (unsound money) monetary system, borrowing and deficits can be exponential due to the ability to inflate the currency.

Below is a simple depiction of the difference between macroeconomics and microeconomics. This is just a general visualization of each strictly for the purpose of an example.

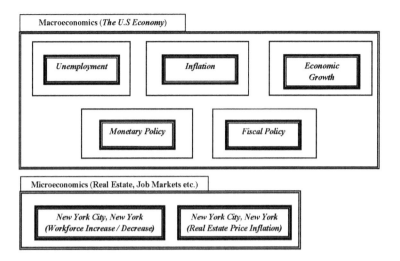

The Economy

Because of our Debt Based Monetary System and the fact that money must be borrowed into existence, our economy is severely flawed and unstable. Our economy's viability is based off of perpetual debt and perpetual growth. Both of these concepts are not sustainable. Perpetual debt means that currency must continue to be borrowed into existence forever, and the currency supply must be perpetually increased through inflation in order for our economy to function and thrive. Any decrease in the money supply (deflation) will inevitably affect our economy in a negative way. If government, people and businesses were not borrowing currency to spend into the economy, then economic growth would come to a crashing halt. Businesses would not be able expand their operations and hire more workers. Underemployment and unemployment would increase. And, worst of all, currency would begin to literally disappear causing all outstanding debts to eventually be defaulted on.

Perpetual growth in a world of limited resources is also unsustainable. We use many natural resources (e.g. oil, land, water and trees) to fuel our economic growth and maintain prominence. Growth cannot be exponential in a system of debt, and a world of limited resources.

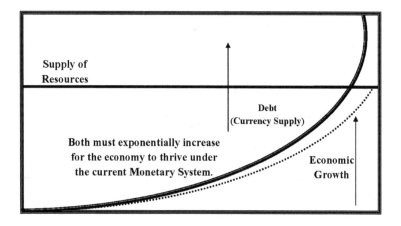

Inflation

Inflation is an increase in the overall money, or currency supply. The Federal Reserve controls the supply of U.S. Dollars available in the national and global economy. They also control the interest rates that must be paid for borrowing our national currency.

Here are a couple of facts about inflation. Any increase in the currency supply is inflation. The currency supply includes Federal Reserve loans to the Government, Bank loans to the public or private institutions, outstanding credit card balances, all derivatives and paper currency in circulation. Inflation makes each currency note in circulation worth less and less, decreasing the purchasing power of each dollar. Inflation is a hidden tax that steals wealth from savers and taxpayers.

Inflation makes banks richer and the public poorer by transferring wealth from the public to the banks.

This **Monetary Inflation Table** shows from year 1 to year 5 how the increase of the overall currency supply by a central bank, or the banking system as a whole, devalues each currency unit, increases cost and therefore lowering the purchasing power of each currency unit (dollar). For "Cost" divide the number of currency units by the number of gold or food units. For "Purchasing Power" divide 1 by the cost. This is for illustration purposes and is not a representation of actual inflation numbers:

Central Bank Currency Units Gold Units Food Units	1,000,000 500,000,000 1,000,000,000	Cost 0.002 (0.21%) 0.001 (0.1%)	**Purchasing Power** 500.00 1,000.00	**Year 1**	
Central Bank **+600,000** Currency Units Gold Units Food Units	1,600,000 500,000,000 1,000,000,000	Cost 0.0032 (0.32%) 0.0016 (0.16%)	**Purchasing Power** 312.50 625.00	**Year 2**	83.87% Decrease of Purchasing Power (Year 1 to Year 5)
Central Bank **+500,000** Currency Units Gold Units Food Units	2,100,000 500,000,000 1,000,000,000	Cost 0.0042 (0.42%) 0.0021 (0.21%)	**Purchasing Power** 238.095 476.19	**Year 3**	16.13% of Initial Purchasing power left
Central Bank **+1,000,000** Currency Units Gold Units Food Units	3,100,000 500,000,000 1,000,000,000	Cost 0.0062 (0.62%) 0.0031 (0.31%)	**Purchasing Power** 161.29 322.58	**Year 4**	
Central Bank **+3,100,000** Currency Units Gold Units Food Units	6,200,000 500,000,000 1,000,000,000	Cost 0.0124 (1.24%) 0.0062 (0.62%)	**Purchasing Power** 80.645 161.29	**Year 5**	

For deflationary effects, you can reverse the table by making year 5 into year 1, working your way up the chart and subtracting each central bank currency increase. Result, the purchasing power on the table will increase.

Debt

Debt is an obligation to repay something borrowed from someone. Most people look at debt as a part of life and a necessity for prosperity. But, here is something most people don't know. Every dollar denomination or Federal Reserve note in circulation is a debt owned back to the Federal Reserve. We operate under a debt based monetary system. This debt is created out of thin air by the exchange of IOUs using Federal Reserve Notes and Government Bonds, or by the signature of a borrower seeking a loan from a bank. This debt is our currency and is supposed to represent value, when in fact there is no value, only debt.

Every dollar in circulation has interest attached to it that must be paid back. Mathematically, this equals an inevitable collapse, because if each dollar must be paid back with interest, where does the money come from to service the interest on each dollar? Answer: It must be borrowed. Our debt based monetary system is a tool of economic slavery, which is meant to keep the masses using their labor to enrich the ones in control.

Our economy is fueled by the concepts of perpetual debt and perpetual growth. Both of these designs are unsustainable. Perpetual debt can never be paid off, because the interest owed on the debt will always outweigh the currency in circulation needed to service that debt. And, perpetual growth in a world of limited resources is unsustainable. Eventually all resources will be depleted or consolidated and growth will cease, causing an economic collapse.

The Petrodollar

In the 1970s, after a series of meetings, a deal was struck

between the Saudi Arabian Royal Family and the United States (represented by Secretary of State, Henry Kissinger), in which the U.S. promised to protect Saudi Arabia from any enemies who may have tried to invade their country and take their oil. The United States also agreed to provide the Saudis with weaponry and "Protection from Israel". In return, the U.S. wanted Saudi oil priced solely in U.S. dollars (meaning to accept only U.S. dollars as payment for their oil), and that the Saudis be open to investing surplus oil proceeds into U.S. bonds. The Saudi's happily agreed. Subsequently, by 1975, the other oil producing OPEC (Organization of the Petroleum Exporting Countries) nations of the Middle East followed suit. It seemed like a good idea at the time because what the U.S. offered was an apparent win-win situation. This transaction made the U.S. dollar the only currency with which you could buy and sell Middle Eastern OPEC crude oil. This gave the U.S. a monopoly on the oil trade and drove up demand for U.S. dollars. The U.S. "Petrodollar" was born making our currency the reserve currency of the world.

Former Iraqi President Saddam Hussein was probably the first head of state in the Middle East to attempt to break from this deal by trading oil for Euros under the Oil for Food Program. We all know what happened to him. In 2003, his country was "liberated" from his alleged tyranny, he was hunted down like a dog, killed and the United States occupied Iraq for 7 years. The U.S. subsequently returned oil sales from the Euros to the Dollar. And to think, he was once an ally of the U.S.

The same fate awaits Iran. They too have been attempting to circumvent the U.S. dollar, because of U.S. (E.U. co-signed) trade sanctions on the country. The U.S. is accusing Iran of so called "Development of Nuclear Weapons" with their developing nuclear program. There has been more evidence indicating that Iran does not have the capability to create nuclear weapons, but the U.S. and Israel are claiming they are gaining the capability. By trading oil for gold and other currencies, Iran is opening up a floodgate. The U.S. and Israel are using the nuclear weapons excuse to eventually invade Iran. This is the same fate that fell upon former Libyan ruler Mohmar Qadhafi. Apparently, he too proposed trading Libyan oil (the 10th largest proven oil reserve in the world) for payment in currencies other than U.S. dollars. He was however covertly removed from power, hunted down like a dog and murdered before he could achieve this. Coincidence, I think not. The fact is that the U.S. will engage in any necessary tactics to preserve the Petrodollar and its world reserve currency status.

Most countries hold U.S. dollar reserves, but more and more countries are beginning to dump more and more U.S. dollars to trade in gold and other local currencies. If more countries dump their dollars, all of that excess cash has to go somewhere. It will all end up back in the United States. That event will most definitely lead to an unspeakable level of hyperinflation. This means that the value of assets, prices of goods and services, and subsequently the cost of living, will rise exponentially. Initially, this will be a good thing for the rich and bad for the middle class. But in the long run, it will lead to hyperinflation and imminent total economic collapse. This is bad for the dollar rich and the middle class, but a great opportunity for those who know how to hedge against it.

Who would stand to benefit the most from the end of the Bretton-Wood system and the creation of the Petrodollar? Think about it. Who controls the supply of dollars and sets the interest rates to borrow those dollars? Think about it. Cui

Bono (means "To Whose Benefit?"). The answer is the Federal Reserve (our Central Bank) and its shareholders.

All central banks are more or less a cartel of the same few international bankers. They indebt the nations they service and the citizens of those nations. They profit and gain power at the expense of the people. There are bankers who hold positions in government. One such example of a banker in government is former New York Federal Reserve President, former U.S. Treasury Secretary and current President of Private Equity Firm Warburg Pincus, Timothy Geithner.

Most of our national and global economic problems are caused by the current debt based monetary system. More specifically, the international bankers who created and perpetuate this system are the problem. They indebt both the people and governments with currency created out of nothing and then take control of assets and resources when debts cannot be paid. They end up consolidating all resources under a smaller group of ownership.

War, humanitarian efforts, taxes, inflation, debt default, control of natural resources and the Petrodollar all have what in common? The banks are the beneficiaries. They fund governments for war efforts, fund humanitarian missions, inflate the currency as needed, fund mining and drilling for resources and benefit from the Petrodollar.

Economic Facts

When the supply of money (i.e. currency) of a country is available in proportion to the production of goods and services in the economy, the currency has value as a means of exchange. People's confidence in a currency as a means of exchange also gives it its value. When the currency supply is inflated (i.e. increased) without a naturally sustained relationship where supply is meeting demand and vice versa, the currency supply becomes devalued.

When demand for goods and services decreases, a surplus is usually created. Prices will decrease to get people to purchase more goods and services. Those goods now have less value due to the abundance. When demand for goods and services increases, a shortage is usually created. Prices will increase because more cash is chasing a limited supply of goods.

When cash is pumped into the economy in an attempt to artificially boost the economy in times of recession, "Bubbles" (or investment booms) are created. This creates the perfect environment for economic disaster and also financial opportunity in the different markets (e.g. real estate or stocks) that the cash is flowing into. Any bubble by design is eventually going to burst, and everything inside of it will plummet. This is what you would call a "Market Crash"; or when cash stops flowing into a market and prices begin to fall drastically. Getting in or out at the right time, or wrong time, can mean the difference between fortune and bankruptcy.

When a monetary system is based on perpetual debt, economic growth cannot be sustained. Consumer debt obligations will eventually exceed their means, and they will inevitably go bankrupt (run out of money). The government's debt obligations will eventually render it insolvent, because the incoming tax revenue will not be enough to satisfy its debt obligation.

When the government's spending exceeds its revenue it is running a budget deficit. To pay for this deficit, the government must borrow money from a central bank, other countries or investors by issuing government bonds (debt instruments).

When the government borrows its own money, at interest,

to fund its own programs, it is basically asking for financial disaster. A country freely giving up control of its monetary policy to outside, or private interests opens up a government to financial disaster and perpetual debt.

Economic Dynamics

Inflation – increase of the money supply: If currency increases (supply), then paper assets decrease (value), precious metals increase (value), commodities increase (value), Cost of living increases (cost), Goods and Services increase (cost), Debt decreases (value), Wages decrease (value) and Tax Revenue decreases (value).

Deflation – decrease of the money supply: If currency decreases (supply), then paper assets increase (value), precious metals decrease (value), commodities decrease (value), Cost of living decreases (cost), Goods and Services decrease (cost), Debt increases (value), Wages increase (value) and Tax Revenue increases (value).

Government Liability – If government employment, expenses and obligations increase, debt increases, taxes must go up to service all debt and obligations. If government employment, expenses and obligations decrease, debt decreases, taxes can remain the same, or decrease. Expanded government obligations require expanded government size, which creates increased government spending and inevitable government deficits and more public debt.

From my understanding, elements that affect our economy have a basic relationship with each other. Any man made imbalance or artificial stimulus will disrupt any natural correction the economy may be able to achieve. If you can understand these dynamics, you can see how artificial our economy has become.

Artificial Economics

The economy is based off of a simple formula of supply and demand. If there is a demand, there must be a supply to meet that demand, and if there is supply, there needs to be a demand to consume that supply. If there is too much supply and not enough demand, a surplus will form and prices will eventually fall. If there is too much demand and not enough supply, then prices will eventually go up to curb consumption, or perhaps increase production to meet the demand. But, prices will go up regardless.

Any type of artificial injection or intervention from the banks or government, in times of recession or collapse is either a stimulus or a bailout. Both a stimulus and a bailout prevent the free market economy (economy unhindered by regulation) from making necessary corrections needed to balance out any bursts, or declines, in the various markets. Quantitative Easing by the Federal Reserve is another form of stimulus in which they increase (inflate) the money supply to provide liquidity, and "stimulate" economic growth. Quantitative Easing doesn't work, because the currency that is pumped into the system goes directly to banks and the financial sector, instead of being directly distributed to the public where it is needed.

Know the Economic Design

The 4 Fundamental Forces

Do you know what the fundamental forces of the Universe are? Most people only know two out of 4 of the fundamental forces of the Universe, and don't even realize the other two exist. These forces control every aspect of cosmic interaction, but also create the very dynamics for creation, as we know it. The four fundamental forces of the Universe, in order of magnitude, consist of Strong Interaction, Electromagnetism,

Weak Interaction and Gravitation.

To briefly explain each, Strong Interaction hold together the atoms of a nucleus, electromagnetism is responsible for magnetism, lightning, friction and phenomena like rainbows, Weak Interactions are responsible for beta decay, also known as radioactivity, or the release of protons and electrons, and Gravitation is responsible for holding celestial bodies in their orbit around other bodies and stars, giving matter with density weight and causing tidal shifts in the oceans and crust.

What does this have to do with anything? Well, these are all forces that you cannot see. You are not even aware of their presence unless it is brought to your attention. You operate within the design of these forces and follow the protocols of these forces. The laws of physics program you. But, what happens when you become aware of these forces like a physicist? What happens when you understand and strive to master these forces? Well, if you can learn how to master them, you can then use them to your advantage and perhaps, discover something that defies these forces.

Humans have done this with gravity. We have discovered ways to travel on air currents using airplanes and helicopters allowing us to fly, and even travel into the vacuum of space with probes and space shuttles. There is even a "Questionable" military weapon called the Laser-Induced Plasma Channel (LIPC) being developed by the U.S. Army, which has harnessed the power of electromagnetism. It can fire a laser guided lightning bolt at a specified target. After splitting atoms to create atomic bombs and controlling nuclear fusion to create nuclear bombs, something like harnessing the power of lightning would eventually become a piece of cake. The point here is to know the forces you are dealing with and you can eventually overcome them.

The Design

How can we master something we cannot see? Well, the effects of the forces tell you that the forces exist and are in control. We cannot see gravity, but we know it exists, because when we trip over something, we fall down; sometimes really hard on our face. Effects show you the forces at work. And if you know the forces exist, you can identify them. Simply ask yourself "What, How and Why" questions about it, and then research it. I guarantee that you will not only find the answers, but you will end up asking yourself other questions about something related to your initial questions. You don't gain applicable knowledge by simply accepting what you are told.

One day in the course of my endless research, I came across a video on a website that spoke about Washington D.C., the City of London and Vatican City being the three City States of the world, which all operate outside of the laws of the countries in which they reside. The video depicted how they control the world through Military Power (D.C.), Financial Control (London) and Spiritual Control (Vatican City).

While viewing this video, I came across a chart. This chart identified the British Royal Control structure of the world. It spoke about the origins of the British Monarchy, and briefly covered their global control structure. This structure basically puts the British Royal Family at the top of the food chain of the world, second only to something symbolized with an eye. The chart showed them having various means of control over the so-called debt slaves (You and I).

The structure of this control system is global, and runs deep in the form of a multi-layer pyramid. This is the hierarchy of the Illuminati, or as some may call them, the New World

Order. Their agenda is to establish a One World Government, One World Monetary System through monetary hyperinflation, economic implosion, resource consolidation, eradication of civil liberties and privacy, socialism and totalitarianism, national disarmament, unifying economies and centralizing control for their own benefit. The hierarchy is as follows:

- The Crown: The governing body of the City of London (Corporation), a committee of 12 banks headed by the House of Rothschild. This committee is the mastermind pulling the strings in the world economy.
- British Monarchy: The Britain Royal Family (House of Windsor). This is the ceremonial crown of Great Britain. This is the one royal family the entire world knows and is considered at the top of the food chain.
- Crown Council of 13: These are the World's Richest, Most Powerful Families, or what some would refer to as the 13 Illuminati Bloodlines (Illuminati), or the enlightened ones. This crown council, or cartel, is comprised of The Astor, The Bundy, The Collins, The DuPont, The Freeman, The Kennedy, The Li, The Onassis, The Reynolds, The Rockefeller, The Rothschild, The Russell and the Van Duyn families. (Do your own research).
- Committee of 300: World's Richest, Most Powerful Sub-families.
- Powerful Sub-families (Think Tanks): This includes The Trilateral Commission, Royal Institute of International Affairs, Club of Rome, Council on Foreign Relations, United Nations and The Builderburg Group; collectively known as The Round Table. These are the groups who determine the direction of world

governments and political events.

- World Financial Control: The International Monetary fund, World Bank, Central Banks and the Bank of International Settlements. These are the controlling groups of world financial and monetary direction. They use Tax Revenue and Interest Revenue to enslave nations and their people.

- World Resource Control: Corporations. These are the entities that gain control over resources and gain wealth through exploitation of human needs, wants and desires.

- World Population Control: This is the mechanism by which the population is kept under strict control. This is achieved through Religions - Teaches heavenly reward for obeying rules, Governments - Secret Service, Military, Police, Courts and Prisons, Education - Programming the intellectual with status quo academia, and Media – Controls the Elite's message to the masses.

- Population Resources = Labor Units: These are the Debts Slaves, or economic slaves who go through the cycle of Birth, School, Labor, Taxes, Debt and Retirement. This is where the 99% are in on the pyramid.

This is the actual Pyramid Structure of the World. Think about it, where do you fall?

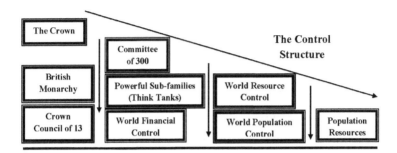

Simply by knowing this design, and the intended effects of it, you know the forces that are working against you. What this means is that The Crown, the Royal Family of Britain, The Committee of 300, those Think Tank Sub-Families, World Financial Institutions, Big Corporations, Religion, Government, Education and The Mainstream Media are all control mechanism forces working against you in a design to keep you an indebted, dependent and subservient subject existing as a resource whose only purpose is to serve the hierarchy of the design. **Note** *Some of these groups have some of the same owners and top ranking members operating within them.*

Just like with gravity holding you down to Earth, all of these forces are holding you down. It's hard to rise above the oppressive, inequality being implemented. Their purpose is to consolidate all resources, establishing a one-world government and global monetary union. But, knowledge is the first key to being able to send a sharp, poisonous spear right up the ass, and through the heart of the so called Monarchy, the richest families, the sub families and all the controlling forces of this pyramid that stand between you and your complete freedom. The way they destroy your freedom is to destroy purchasing power via inflation, create economic slaves through debt and interest, and destroy civil liberties through socialism.

Economic Physics

Allow me to lay out some of the physics of economics. Understanding this can at least give you some piece of mind in knowing why the economy is the way it is. And, at best, this information can make you financially independent if you apply the knowledge you gain in a constructive and responsible way. Here are a few points of the physics of economics.

You rarely hear about deflation in the economy. Most of the talk is about monetary inflation and subsequent price inflation. Well I'm going to explain what happens when the economy experiences deflation.

First, deflation is a decrease in the overall money (currency) supply. This occurs when outstanding credit card debt, car loans, mortgages and other debts are paid off. Remember, currency is debt. When these debts are satisfied, the currency created from those debts disappears. The less currency circulating in the economy, the more value each dollar in circulation holds. Theoretically, each dollar can now purchase more goods and services, because of the increased value. This means that paper assets go up in value too. However, gold, silver and other commodities go down in value, because it takes fewer dollars to acquire these commodities.

If the currency is going up in value and you can buy more with your cash, the cost of goods and services go down, as does the cost of living. Debt becomes more valuable and profitable, because each dollar is worth more. Theoretically, wages will go up, because it cost less for business to pay employees. Income taxes will go down, because it takes less taxpayer dollars to satisfy current government obligations.

In an Inflationary economy, the money (currency) supply would increase; probably due to Federal Reserve imposing quantitative easing or lowering interest rates to stimulate the economy. An increase in the supply of currency would devalue each dollar in circulation, reducing the purchasing power thereof. Paper assets become worth less and less, adding more risk to investing in them. Gold, silver and other commodities go up in value because it now takes more dollars to purchase them.

The influx of cash causes the price of goods and services to increase, therefore making the cost of living higher. Debt becomes less valuable and profitable, because each dollar is worth less, so lenders don't make the same returns as in a more deflationary economy. Theoretically, wages go down because it cost more for businesses to pay employees. Income taxes will go up, because 1. Inflation is a hidden tax on the middle class and 2. It takes more taxpayer dollars to satisfy future government debt obligations.

If you factor in government reducing the number of employees it has on payroll, therefore lowering its payroll expenses and the amount of cash it must spend to operate, and consequently borrow from the banks, then taxes would go down as well. Government would require less capital expenditure on salaries for government jobs, which don't produce any economic goods or services. Fewer taxes paid to the government means more cash for consumers to spend into the economy. Subsequently, that means more cash available for businesses to hire people. But, instead of working towards this, the government is doing the exact opposite and working against the positive physics of the economy.

Conclusion

The forces of nature are all around us. But, the forces that wish to control our lives and prosperity are also all around us, watching and manipulating. We must make a conscious effort to understand factors that affect our economy, our debt based monetary system, our corrupt financial system and our conflicted, revolving door government. By understanding the dynamics of these forces and the systems that control various aspects of our lives, we can then use them to our advantage, and beat them; or we can simply dismantle them and create a new, fairer system.

Predict the Financial Future

The 7 Steps

A few years ago, I had come across some information that caught my attention. This information stated something that appears to elude the middle class before an impending economic collapse. This information may seem like something extraordinary, but it is actually very simple. This information consists of a pattern that has repeated in many parts of the world, with different powerful empires, throughout history.

And, resulting in today's impending economic collapse, The United States of America has followed this same pattern, or cycle. We are now at the end of a cycle that will forever change this country. This cycle will not destroy the wealth of the middle class, but rather transfer it to those who hold the correct assets when the collapse happens. This pattern, or cycle is what investor Mike Maloney refers to as the "7 Steps Used by the Ultra Rich to Predict the Financial Future". These 7 steps are as follows:

- Good Money
- Social Programs
- Military Spending
- War
- Inflation
- Wealth Transfer

Good Money (1) – If you hear the term "Good Money" some people may relate it to being alright, straight or doing well. But, in the context of this book, that is not the case. Good Money refers to how a country's monetary system starts out. A country usually starts out with money that is gold, or backed by gold. This money cannot be manipulated, created out of thin air or artificially inflated. This is what one would call "honest money" or "Sound Money", because it is in the form of a natural resource, or is backed by a natural resource. The money is limited by the quantity of the resource.

Social Programs (2) – As a nation becomes more and more developed in its economy and social status, it undertakes various public works and social program initiatives that add to the financial strain of the nation. With all of the social programs of our nation (e.g. Social Security, Medicaid/ Medicare/

Welfare/ Food Stamps), the government has spent billions of dollars each year on these entitlements. As of December 1, 2013, the U.S. Government had unfunded liabilities totaling $126.78 Trillion; $16.71 Trillion is Social Security and $87.95 Trillion is Medicare. How can they sustain that with only $2.81 Trillion in revenue? Answer, they cannot.

Military Spending (3) – Economic growth of a country begins to foster its political power. With political power comes the need to protect its national interest. Protecting a country's national interest requires expenditures for military expansion. We all know government spending for the military can reach astronomical levels as it did during the Iraqi War. The current defense budget is approximately $603.59 Billion.

War (4) – That last point brings me to number four; once a country begins spending on military and defense, it is only a matter of time before that country puts its military to use.

Fiat Currency (5) – In order to finance the expenditures of an expanding military and defense, and the ongoing obligations of war, the government starts to steal the wealth of the people by issuing a currency in place of money. This means that the country can now inflate the currency to unlimited proportions to fund its wars and other expenditures.

Inflation (6) – When the currency supply is expanded to such proportions that it causes prices to rise continuously and the cost of living to increase to the point of poverty, people feel the effects of their savings and earnings not having the same purchasing power as before. This causes people to begin to lose faith in the currency and the system. As with today, more and more people are seeing the monetary and financial systems for the fraud they are, and are becoming more knowledgeable about how to protect themselves from banks.

Wealth Transfer (7) – Once the people lose faith in the

currency, they begin moving their remaining wealth out of the currency in masses and into precious metals (i.e. gold and silver). You can call it a sell-off of the currency. Once this happens, the currency ultimately collapses and massive amounts of wealth are transferred to those who had the insight and knowledge to convert their currency holdings into the appropriate asset class before the collapse. Our nation, as well as the European Union, is on the verge of a massive wealth transfer that cannot be avoided. The only question is which side of the wealth transfer will you be on?

Which Side Will You Be On?

The United States currently sits between stages 6 and 7. We are on the verge of hyperinflation, which will destroy the purchasing power of our currency, causing its inevitable demise, and the collapse of our economy. While this seems like a runaway train heading for the end of the tracks, with all of us on it, will you know when the right time is to jump off before the train crashes at the end? Do you even know how to prepare yourself to get off this runaway train? Do you know how to protect yourself from this disaster? The sad and honest truth is that most people don't even realize that there is an end coming. Most people will ride this economic train until it hits the end. They will be most affected by the crash. While people like me are preparing to jump off before the crash, most people will ultimately be severely hurt by what is coming.

Challenges Ahead: There are 3 challenges that we face

New Debt – In our debt based monetary system and economy, deflation is a bigger enemy than inflation. With deflation, money is destroyed; meaning the supply decreases and therefore the economy slows down. Our government will do everything within its power to keep deflation from spiraling out of control. So, our government takes on more and more debt, borrowing from the private Federal Reserve to keep the perpetual debt engine running. But, our country also has countries like China that are a huge creditor of the U.S., but has begun selling off our debt. This is because countries around the world are seeing the U.S. government's fiscal policy for what it is; Simply Bad. This means that countries will start to sell off U.S. debt and U.S. currency. This will also lead to hyperinflation. So now, the Federal Reserve, being the lender of last resort, is forced to purchase this debt. This is what you call "Debt Monetization". That means the Federal Reserve has to print (or create) more currency out of thin air, to buy this debt; which our government must pay interest on. Oh yeah, that interest is paid through taxpayers' dollars. The more interest that is owed on this debt means more currency must be created. That means more debt is inevitably owed.

If you ever heard about the U.S. debt ceiling, that topic plays a huge role in the U.S. economy as well. If for some reason the U.S. didn't raise the debt ceiling, or the U.S. simply defaulted on its debt obligations, the U.S. would lose its current AA+ credit rating, causing all interest rates on our government's debt to dramatically increase. All borrowing cost would rise, the housing market would be destroyed and all paper assets (e.g. stocks, mutual funds and 401k plans) would crash. That's just the tip of the iceberg. All government workers (which make up at least 50% of the U.S. workforce) would stop receiving their paychecks and government dependents would stop receiving their benefits. That means the government must perpetually increase the debt ceiling to keep the economy going. The only problem is an economy with limited resources cannot sustain itself off of perpetual growth and perpetual debt.

Social Entitlements Obligations – We are entering a period in our history where retiring adults are going to be cashing in on their social entitlements (e.g. Social Security and Medicare). This means that the government must payout benefits to all of these people looking for their government entitlements. The problem with that is the government has a $17.20 Trillion debt, but only $2.81 Trillion in income. Plus, the government has unfunded liabilities totaling $126.78 Trillion; $16.71 Trillion is Social Security liabilities and $87.95 Trillion is Medicare.

This system is a disaster waiting to happen. There are only two possible solutions, 1. Inflate the currency supply by printing more currency to reduce the overall value of the unfunded liabilities to manageable levels, and dilute the value of all currency already in existence causing prices to rise from the inflation, or 2. Simply default on the debt. The government isn't going to default on a debt when they basically have a blank check from The Federal Reserve to keep creating more money.

Great 401k Pullout – This was a prediction of Investor Robert Kiyosaki, which he wrote in his book "Rich Dad Prophecy". When Social Security was created in 1935, there were 42 workers for every retiree. Today there are only 3.3 workers. By 2030, there will only be 2 workers for every retiree, which means it will be impossible to continue funding the Social Security program.

Baby-boomers (people born during the Post-World War II baby boom era 1946 to 1964) have a little surprise underway for the economy called the IRA, or Individual Retirement Account. This surprise ensures that the biggest stock market crash in history is now impending. Congress created the 401k plan in 1974 as an attempt to fix the dying pension system.

Since then, the 401k, and IRA's have become the primary vehicle for investing the money of the Boomers into the stock
market. Their massive population combined with relatively
steady times in the U.S. politically and financially, created
immense demand for stocks and mutual funds. Today, the majority of wealth in the U.S. is held by baby-boomers in their
retirement accounts. But, a small technicality is going to trigger the biggest crash in history. As these boomers reach age
65 between 2012 and 2016, the law requires them to pull out
approximately 6% of their money out each year, which will
begin the forced sale of their stock holdings. This means that
the largest and richest group of people in the country will pull
their cash out of the stock market at the same time.

Younger generations won't be able to purchase the same
amount of stock being sold by the forced sale of the boomers
stock. So, prices will begin to drop quickly. As retiree's see
the value of their retirement dropping day after day, they will
instinctively pull their remaining cash out sooner, which will
start a frenzy of people exiting the market. This will provide
an opportunity for savvy investors.

How to Protect Yourself

In all of this economic, monetary and financial chaos,
there is a tremendous opportunity out there. The situation is
extremely scary, but for those who decide to understand the
situation and take advantage of the opportunities presented,
they will come out on top of this event in better shape than
they went into it. Do not hide under a rock and be ignorant to
the realities of the economy. A huge wealth transfer is about
to take place. What side of it are you going to be on?

We are in a deflationary stage with the housing and credit
markets. This means that debts owed on houses are still being

defaulted on, or have gone into foreclosure. Remember, when a debt is not being serviced, the money that was created out of thin air (or a signature to be precise) disappears and vanishes back into thin air where it came from. So, if debts owed on housing are not being serviced, banks are not going to continue to issue credit as frequently due to outstanding loans and accumulating losses.

The Federal Reserve (our Central Bank) will most likely continue to print vast amounts of currency (QE3 and QE Infinity) to bring us out of this deflationary stage. This will begin to send us into a hyperinflationary stage. Once this happens, the free market will begin to automatically adjust the prices of goods, services and commodities. Gold and silver, the only true money will start to account for all the new U.S. currency printed and will rise in value against the dollar.

What does that mean to the average person?

All the dollars you have accumulated through savings will eventually be worth less than they are today. The only way to preserve your purchasing power of today is to convert your dollar denominated savings into the right asset class. I will discuss these asset classes in the Ultimate Economic Hedge section below.

Know Asset Protection

Limited Liability

Asset Protection is a method or process in which you protect personal assets from business and other liability. Through the process of forming a legal business entity or incorporation, you can begin to establish your limited liability and create what is called a corporate veil. This veil keeps creditors from being able to go after your personal assets in the event your business is sued or goes bankrupt. This is an important asset protection tool. You must understand that:

Limited liability pertains to the protection granted by law that limits your personal liability to the extent of your investment into a business venture or partnership. Your personal assets are not at risk, unless you are knowingly and willingly involved in fraud or negligent acts in some way.

The way to gain limited liability is to form a legal entity and do business solely under, and in the name of that entity. Never combine your personal accounts and expenses with that of your business. Follow this and you should never be personally liable for any obligations in the business's name.

Incorporation

The definition of incorporation is consolidating two or more things into one union, or one body. This is basically saying two or more people or entities converge to form one entity. In the business world, incorporation is what one or more people do to form a new legal entity to carry out business operations. When someone incorporates, they file what is known as Articles of Incorporation, or Articles of Organization, with their respective state's Secretary of the Department of State, and then file for an Employer Identification Number (EIN) with the IRS. Once this is completed, all business is conducted in and under the name of the new entity. All accounts for the new entity are in the entity's name under the entity's EIN. By law, the owners of the entity are afforded "limited liability" and are not personally liable for any of the business's obligations, unless fraud is involved.

There are various forms of business entities one can form, but not all of them afford the benefit of limited liability. Based on the goals of the owners and the type of business venture, you must decide the type of entity you want to form. *These are the different entities*:

C Corporation (Inc.): This is a standard corporation that is taxed at the corporate level and the shareholder level. The C Corporation can have an unlimited number of shareholders. Shareholders need not be citizens of the United States to own a C Corporation. Shares of a C Corporation can be publicly traded. C Corporations must elect a board of directors and keep corporate minutes.

S Corporation (Inc.): This is a sub-chapter S corporation. S Corporations start out as C Corporations and the owners must elect to be taxed as an S Corporation by filing papers with the IRS. All profits and losses are passed through to the owners who then claim the profits or losses on their personal income. S Corporations can only have a maximum of 100 shareholders and they must be citizens of the United States.

Professional Corporation (PC): This is simply a Corporation that is owned by a professional who has a specialty (e.g. Doctor, Lawyer, Dentist or Architect).

Limited Liability Company (LLC): This is a legal entity (not a corporation) that is separate from the owners like a corporation, but all profits and losses are passed through to the owners. LLCs can be taxed as either a partnership or sole proprietorship. LLCs don't elect a board of directors since LLC Members (owners) manage the business and they don't have to keep corporate minutes. Ownership in an LLC is called "percentage interest" or can be called a "unit". There is no set number of owners for LLCs.

Limited Partnership (LP): This is a partnership that has one or more general partners and one or more limited partners. General partners control the limited partnership and all of its assets, but have unlimited personal liability for the limited partnership's obligations. Limited partners do not and cannot manage any of the affairs of the business. If they do, they become liable as a general partner. As long as limited partners don't take part in the day-to-day affairs of the business, they are afforded limited liability. Limited partners also aren't required to be publicly identified as an owner. All profits and losses are passed through to the partners. Ownership is usually expressed as a percentage.

Family Limited Partnership (LP): This is simply a family owned limited partnership.

General Partnership: This is a partnership between two or more persons. All partners are personally liable for the obligations of the business, whether they incurred them or not. General partnerships can be formed without any formal paperwork. All profits and losses are passed through to the owners.

Sole Proprietorship: This is a business owned by one person. The owner is personally liable for the obligations of the business. All profits and losses are passed through to the owner.

Limited Liability Partnership (LLP): This is a General partnership where some or all of the partners are afforded limited liability under appropriate state authority.

Master Limited Partnership (MLP): This is a limited partnership that is publicly traded like a corporation.

Notary Services

Notaries Public can be essential partners for businesses and individuals in preventing fraud and legitimizing written instruments, certain transactions and proof of identity. Notaries Public are empowered by the Secretary of State to administer oaths (verbal pledges) and affirmations (solemn declarations) for affidavits (signed statement, duly sworn to) and depositions (testimony of a witness taken out of court).

They can also perform acknowledgments of written instruments (formal declaration that one has executed a written instrument and such execution is their act and deed), take proofs by subscribing witnesses (formal declaration by subscribing witness to the execution of an instrument, setting forth their place of residence, that they know the person in and who executed the instrument, and they saw such person execute such instrument), demand payment/ acceptance of written obligations (bills of exchange, promissory notes etc) and witness safe deposit box openings.

Notaries are also good to use for field verification of residency or specific assets. Those certified to do so can also administer document signing as a Notary Signing Agent.

Limited Partnerships

A Limited Partnership (LP) is a partnership that has one or more general partners and one or more limited partners. General partners control the limited partnership and all of its assets, but have unlimited personal liability for the limited partnership's obligations. Limited partners do not and cannot manage any of the affairs of the business. If they do, they become liable as a general partner. As long as limited partners don't take part in the day to day affairs of the business, they are afforded limited liability and are not required to be publicly identified as an owner. All profits and losses are passed through to the partners. Since general partners are personally liable for the obligations of the business, the best way to set up a limited partnership is:

- To have a corporation act as the general partner holding 1% ownership interest in the company. Creditors cannot force dissolution of the limited partnership if the general partner only owns 1% equity.

- Then, have the general partners of the limited partnership manage the day to day affairs of the limited partnership through the corporation without being personally liable. This keeps the liability on the entity and allows the real managing individuals to be shielded from personal liability.
- And the limited partners, who can also be the managers (i.e. officers) of the general partner corporation, can collectively hold the remaining 99% ownership interest without their ownership interest being at risk. If the limited partnership is sued, a creditor can get what is called a charging order against the limited partnership. The general partners must pay the creditor with any distributions received. This works against the creditor to the fact that they get taxed as if they received money, even if they didn't. The general partner can choose to refrain from making distributions to itself.
- Only place safe assets into the limited partnership and hold dangerous assets under other entities (i.e. an LLC). Safe assets (e.g. business interest, stock certificates, cash, brokerage accounts, bank accounts) don't bring the risk of being sued upon the owner. Dangerous assets bring the risk of being sued upon the owner (e.g. Real Estate, Equipment).

NOTE: This is purely based on my research, findings and experience, and is strictly my recommendation. This is not to be considered legal advice.

Gold/ Silver Investing

One of the biggest financial opportunities in today's economic situation is investing in precious metals; namely gold and silver. Our economy is heading towards a massive change. In this change, there is going to be a huge transfer of wealth. How? The Federal Reserve continues to create vast amounts of our currency, inflating the currency supply, and therefore, decreasing the purchasing power of the U.S. dollar. Because of this inflation, people who save and hoard U.S. dollars are going to be on the losing end of this transfer. Their savings, and purchasing power, is going to be wiped out. Confidence in the U.S. dollar is fading around the world. The only safe haven away from a failing currency throughout history has been gold and silver.

Precious metals such as gold and silver are excellent investments as currencies rise and fall continuously, because:

Gold and silver are always valuable forms of money (it's in the U.S. Constitution).

When (not if) a currency loses some of its purchasing power, your monetary value will always be secure in gold and silver. Gold and Silver preserves your wealth, and keeps it from becoming a casualty of hyperinflation or economic collapse.

Gold and silver are good ways to diversify your assets (NOTE: Always purchase physical gold and silver. If you can't hold it, you don't own it).

Physical Gold and Silver provide privacy. Banks don't control your wealth when you own physical gold and silver as they do with dollar deposits, and government cannot pry into any accounts to see how much wealth you hold.

Remember This

True wealth isn't measured by how much currency (a.k.a. money) you have in the bank. True (natural) wealth is measured in abundance... that is abundance of natural resources and commodities. True money can only come in the form of gold and silver. Our currency is only an accepted medium in which to acquire these things. It's not the real wealth.

Asset Classes

Asset Classes

Knowing ways in which to protect your assets is vital to financial independence and protecting what you have established. But, you cannot protect an asset properly if you do not know what type of asset it is and how it affects your financial statement (balance sheet, income statement and cashflow statement). There are effectively 9 types of assets that affect your financial statement in various ways. The 9 types of assets are equities, debentures, derivatives, real property, intellectual property, businesses, precious metals, currencies and insurance.

Equities consist of stock or units of ownership held in a publicly traded, or privately held, corporation or company. Equities are basically some form of equity or ownership claim on an asset and rights to any distributions or capital gains accumulated during your time of ownership. Equities also include exchange traded funds (ETFs) and mutual funds.

Debentures are any type of debt instrument. A debt instrument is some form of promise to pay created between a creditor (the lender) and a debtor (the borrower). Debentures include, but aren't limited to, secured and unsecured notes and government, municipal and corporate bonds.

Derivatives are any type of contract that places a claim on an underlying asset, for a specified period of time, without actually owning the underlying asset. Derivatives basically allow you to control an asset, or lay claim to certain rights of an asset, without the obligation of having to exercise your rights. Usually selling a derivative pays you a premium, but obligates you to take on risk, where buying a derivative coasts you cash, but allows you to shift the downside risk to another party. Derivatives include options, futures, collateralized debt obligations and mortgage backed securities.

Real property includes any type of real estate or land, plus any fixed or attached structures like buildings, warehouses or residential homes. Holding title to a property entitles you to the right to sell or lease the property to others, or even license or sell specific right such as air or mineral rights.

Intellectual property is basically any idea developed into a tangible medium that becomes the exclusive property of the creator upon creation. This can be exploited for profit through publishing, licensing and other exclusive rights granted to the owner of the intellectual property. Intellectual property includes copyrights, trademarks, trade secrets and patents.

Business is any commercial venture undertaken for profit. In a business, you provide some type of product or service to people or other businesses and manage your income and expenses effectively enough to turn a profit.

Precious metals include gold and silver bullion, which is investment grade metal. These precious metals can be used as hedges against inflation and a means to protect your savings and purchasing power. Precious metals are probably the safest way to accumulate your savings, because it is safe from the prying eyes of government and bank manipulation.

Currency, or cash, is basically the dollars, Euros, Yen, Yuan or any other paper central bank note printed by a government, and given value by government decree, that you can hold in your hand and spend into the economy. They have no intrinsic value, but are used as a medium of exchange for goods and services.

You may not consider insurance as an asset based on this list, but depending on the type of insurance, you just may have an asset in your portfolio. All insurance cost you money regardless if you file a claim or not, and most of them don't pay you for being a policyholder. Well, there is one type of insurance that pays you for being a policyholder, provides financial leverage and compounded returns all in one policy. I will reveal the details later, but insurance can be a powerful asset to add to your portfolio.

Taking the time to understand how each of these assets work, and how they generate cashflow, add to your net worth, or preserve your wealth, can help you to create a financial fortress and establish a financial legacy, which you can leave to your family.

Ultimate Economic Hedge

Ultimate Economic Hedge (UEH)

We all face the inevitable forces of taxes, debt, inflation, and retirement. Because of our current monetary system and the ever-increasing necessity to expand debt, these forces are inescapable. Were some of us may know how to use these forces to our advantage, the majority of people sadly are victims to these forces. They are economic slaves who sell their labor in exchange for artificial representations of value. While selling your services, or labor, for a wage is not bad, relying solely on one paycheck to secure your financial future is insane. This is true, especially when you factor in taxes, debt, inflation, and retirement costs. Through my research, I have discovered what I would call the "Ultimate Economic Hedge" or UEH against taxes, debt, inflation and retirement.

This UEH covers all bases for financial independence, wealth creation and wealth preservation, from establishing the foundation of your wealth to the fruition of your Financial Fortress (or what I call the World's Best Business). Through methods that involve unconventional ways to extract wealth from the stock market (yes, the stock market) and using the true wealth of human and natural resources to secure your hard earned monetary value, I have discovered the Ultimate Economic Hedge.

The UEH is also a low overhead, simple strategy for investing, owning businesses, and acquiring other assets, without incurring huge amounts of the risks and liability. This is an income producing, low risk hedge against taxes, debt, inflation and retirement. The Ultimate Economic Hedge is comprised of 7 investment strategies that fall within 3 systems. You will learn the 7 amazing strategies now and 3 systems momentarily. The 7 strategies include:

- Incorporation – *Knowing how to protect your assets, isolate liability and form legal entities.*
- Capital Gains – *Knowing how to generate instant cash with, and from, every transaction.*
- Passive Income – *Knowing how to create a passive monthly income from equity and debt.*
- Compounded Returns – *Knowing how to create inflation beating, exponential returns.*

- Hyperinflation Hedge – *Knowing how to hedge against inflation; protect purchasing power.*
- Value Appreciation – *Knowing how to increase value with a tax free strategy.*
- Family Banking System – *Knowing how to create your own private banking system.*

Incorporation

By forming a legal entity, you effectively and strategically shield your personal assets from any litigation that may result from business operations. Through a legal concept called a corporate veil, which separates business owners from the legal entity, the owners of a corporation, limited partners of a limited partnership or members of an LLC are afforded what is known as limited liability. Incorporation, or forming a legal entity, protects you from full liability. This means you are only liable to the extent of your investment in a business, and all of your personal assets are protected from business liability. As long as you don't co-mingle personal and business assets, the corporate veil usually cannot be pierced. But, by forming multiple legal entities for different business operations, you can isolate different levels of liability from others.

When you incorporate, you create a separate legal entity, which can own its own assets and incur liability in its own name. This distinguishes the entity from its owners. All accounts and transactions are in the name of the separate legal entity.

Legal entities can be established for any lawful purpose. They can be created for the purpose of executing business operations, or solely for holding assets. Because a legal entity does not physically interact with people, but can do business and own assets in its own name, they are a great way to separate your name from any property which could bring litigation upon you, or could be in danger of being taken through your own personal liabilities. Assets should be controlled through legal entities and not personally owned by individuals. With the exclusion of maybe one or two small bank accounts, it's reasonably unsafe to hold a substantial amount of assets in your name.

Business which incurs, or carries, high liabilities should be conducted through properly constructed Limited Liability Companies, C Corporations, or Limited Partnership entities with a C Corporation as the general partner (GP). Properly constructing your entity and following all legal formalities (e.g. state filings, minutes, and tax filings) should keep you from incurring any personal liability.

A legal entity can be used for holding personal assets (valuable, safe assets), holding business assets or conducting business operations. Learning tricks and tips to setting up the proper entity for your situation, establishing limited liability and protecting your assets are vital. Before you begin acquiring assets, or doing business, you must establish a foundation. Incorporation, or creating a legal entity, is that foundation to your financial fortress.

Capital Gains

The stock market... Most people get nervous when they hear the word stock market. Most people don't understand how to properly invest in the stock market. When people invest in the stock market, they usually try to buy a "hot stock" when it's perceived to be undervalued, and try to sell it when it goes up. The problem with that is, you are basically gambling with your cash. And, a majority of the time, you stand to lose more than you can possibly gain. For that, you might as well buy a couple hundred dollars worth of lottery tickets, because you are playing with the same type of dangerous speculation.

When uneducated people invest in the stock market, they often buy a stock at the market price hoping it will appreciate in value, or they set a limit price, and wait for it their order to be executed. Both of these strategies set you up for failure. You either win or you lose. Those are your only two options. But, there is a better and more advantageous way to play the stock market. And it truly gives you options.

By trading a derivative of a security (i.e. stock) called an Option, you can effectively place yourself in a win-win-win situation. How can you be in a win-win-win situation in the stock market? Well, for one, it's the options market, and two, I'll explain here. By trading two simple types of options, namely naked puts and covered calls, on World Dominating Dividend Growers (WDDG), Master Limited Partnerships (MLP), publicly traded Real Estate Investment Trusts (REIT), Business Development Companies (BDC) and fundamentally sound Corporations (CORP), you can virtually create money out of thin air with little capital output, and little risk other than the obligation to buy, or sell, the underlying asset in the event the option is exercised.

In the options market, an option is an agreement to buy or sell 100 shares of a security (i.e. a stock or ETF) at an agreed upon price, within an agreed upon time, if the security trades above (call option), or below (put option), the agreed upon strike price by the agreed upon date (or expiration date). The seller of the option is obligated to buy (put option) or sell (call option) if the option is exercised by the buyer. The seller receives a premium for selling the option. If the option is not exercised the seller keeps the whole premium. This can be repeated multiple times.

As banks sell fraudulent, toxic derivatives into the financial markets, they create huge counterparty risk for others and themselves; all while getting rich in the process. Trading options is a legitimate way to sell an insurance policy to a position holder, or prospective position holder, and earn cash in the process. You would be essentially selling derivatives just like the big banks, but without the huge risk, toxic debt or fraudulent & deceptive practices.

How does it work? Let's say you want to own shares of X-Y-Z stock, but X-Y Z stock is currently trading at $10.00 a share. You feel that $10.00 a share is too expensive and you want to buy the stock at a price you agree is more reasonable. You decide that you wouldn't mind owning X-Y-Z stock at $8.50 a share. So, instead of waiting for X-Y-Z stock to go from $10.00 down to $8.50, you click on the stock's option chain and view the available options on X-Y-Z stock. After evaluating the options chain, you decide to sell a put option on X-Y-Z stock with a strike price of $8.50 and an expiration date of January 1, 2015. For the purpose of this example, this particular option has a bid price of $1.00 and expires next month. What does this mean? This means that if you execute (sell) this particular option, you will receive a payment called a premium in the amount of $1.00 for obligating yourself to buy X-Y-Z stock at $8.50, if it trades below $8.50, after expiration.

That's how it works, but here are the rules. A put option is a contract that gives the buyer the right, but not the obligation, to sell 100 shares of a stock if the stock falls below an agreed upon price (strike price) by a specified date (expiration date). A put option is a contract that pays a premium to the seller for taking on the obligation to buy 100 shares of a stock if the stock falls below an agreed upon price by a specified date.

So, X-Y-Z Stock Put Option Symbol would look like this: XYZ010120158.5P, or XYZJan0120158.5Put. The bid (or sell) price would appear next to the corresponding ask (or buy) price. The bid is usually less than the ask price. At $1.00 per share, your premium (or payment) would be $100, because each options contract controls 100 shares of a stock. If you decide to sell 10 contracts, you would receive a $1,000 premium for a 1,000 share obligation, obligating you to $8,500 of X-Y-Z stock, if X-Y-Z stock trades below the $8.50 strike price, after expiration (remember 100 shares = $850, so 1,000 shares = $8,500). With a cash-secured option trade, this cash would be placed into an escrow with your broker until after the expiration date. After the expiration date, one of two things will happen, a) the stock goes up or stays about the same, you keep the premium as profit and your cash is credited back to your account, or b) you purchase shares of XYZ at the strike price with the cash in escrow. In reality, you paid $7,500 for stock you agreed to pay $8,500 for, because of the premium you received upfront. That is a great deal and an excellent trade. Although your premium could be slightly reduced due to commission, contract cost and brokerage fees, you can still come out on top if the premium is high enough, or you are trading multiple contracts.

A call option is a contract that gives the buyer the right, but not the obligation, to buy 100 shares of a stock if the stock goes above an agreed upon price (strike price) by a specified date (expiration date). A call option is a contract that pays a premium to the seller for taking on the obligation to sell 100 shares of a stock if the stock goes above an agreed upon price by a specified date. For this example, you already own X-Y-Z stock.

So, X-Y-Z Stock Call Option Symbol would look like this:

XYZ0101201510.0C or XYZJan01201510.0Call. The bid (or sell) price would appear next to the corresponding ask (or buy) price. In this case, whether you own a 1000 share position in X-Y-Z stock, or not (no position is naked), you the seller would receive a premium for selling the right to buy X-Y-Z stock, let's say at a $10.00 (strike price) for example, if X-Y-Z stock trades above $10.00 after the expiration date. Assuming X-Y-Z has the same $1.00 bid, one of three things happens here, a) you keep the $1,000 premium as profit and you keep the stock you own the position in, or you don't have to cover the stock you sold the naked (no position) call on, b) you are force to sell the stock at the strike price, but keep the $1,000 premium and any capital gains, or c) you must cover (or buy) the stock to be sold at the current market price, and suffer a loss. Covered calls are a better choice to reduce risk.

Math is one of my least favorite subjects in the world. But, math can help us understand some seemingly complex equations that words can distort. Below is an algebraic depiction of the process of selling both put options and call options. I wanted to create a reference for selling both put options and call options that hopefully wouldn't confuse anyone. To better understand the process of how the put option and call option work, follow the formulas below.

Put Option / Call Option

c = 100 / n = Quantity of c / b = Bid / s = Strike Price / p = Premium / tc = Total \$ Amount to be Covered / cc = Commission & Contract Cost / ac = Actual Cost / pp = Put Profit / roc = Return of Capital (not profit)	*c = 100 / n = Quantity of c / b = Bid / s = Strike Price / p = Premium / ts = Total \$ Amount to be Sold / bp = Buy Price / sp = Sell Price / cc = Commission & Contract Cost / ac = Actual Cost / cp = Call Profit*
$b \times (c \times n) = p$	
$s \times (c \times n) = tc$	$s \times (c \times n) = ts$
$(tc + cc^1) - (p - cc^2) = ac$ (exercised)	$(ts - bp - cc^2) + (p - cc^1) = ac$ (-) or cp (+) (exercised) (uncovered)
$p - cc = pp$ (not exercised)	$(p - cc^1) + (sp - bp - cc^2) = cp$ (exercised) (covered)
$tc = roc$ (not exercised)	$p - cc = cp$ (not exercised)

Note: c represents 1 option contract. 1st cc is for option transaction; 2nd cc is for cover transaction.

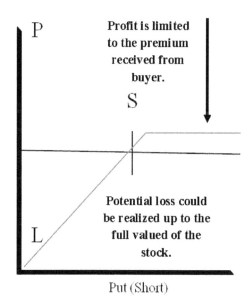

Put (Short)

The Short Put chart shows how your profit is limited to the amount of the premium you receive from the buyer. It is limited, because you are receiving a payment upfront for taking on the obligation, and risk, of buying the shares at the strike price, if the stock is trading below the strike price at the expiration date.

If you are forced to purchase the stock and for some reason the stock continues to plummet, you could lose up to the entire value you paid for the stock. Although this is very unlikely to happen, especially if you are trading options on WDDG and other fundamentally sound businesses, you are inherently getting paid to take on risk.

Good if you think the price will rise or stay the same.

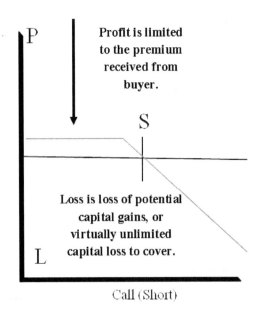

Profit is limited to the premium received from buyer.

S

Loss is loss of potential capital gains, or virtually unlimited capital loss to cover.

P

L

Call (Short)

The Short Call chart shows how your profit is limited to the amount of the premium you receive from the buyer. It is limited, because you are receiving a payment upfront for taking on the obligation, and risk, of selling the shares at the strike price, if the stock is trading above the strike price at the expiration date.

If you are forced to sell the stock, and through some stroke of bad luck the stock continues to rise, you will lose out on the potential capital gains accumulating from the stock price appreciating. That's on covered calls. If you sold a naked call, you could see virtually unlimited capital losses from being forced to buy the stock at the current price and selling at the strike price.

Good if you think the price will fall or stay the same.

Conversely, if you were to buy options, your losses would be limited to the premium you pay to the seller. But, if you buy a put, your profits are either locked in, or your losses are minimized. If you buy a call, your profits are virtually unlimited.

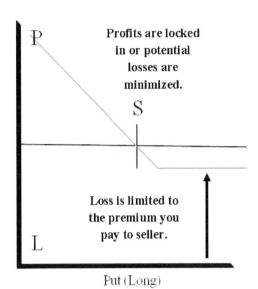

Profits are locked in or potential losses are minimized.

Loss is limited to the premium you pay to seller.

Put (Long)

The Long Put chart shows how your losses are limited to the premium you pay to the seller. It is limited, because you are essentially paying the seller to take on the risk of purchasing your stock at the strike price, if it trades below the strike price at the expiration date.

If for some reason the stock begins to plummet below the strike price, you can exercise your right to sell the stock to the seller of the put option and either lock in your capital gains, or minimize any losses you may suffer from the drop in share price. This is good insurance for an investor who has accumulated a substantial amount of capital gains, or could suffer losses if the stock price falls.

Good if you think the stock price will fall.

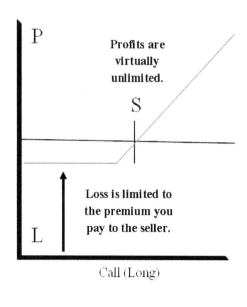

Profits are virtually unlimited.

S

Loss is limited to the premium you pay to the seller.

Call (Long)

The Long Call chart shows how your losses are limited to the premium you pay to the seller. It is limited, because you are essentially paying the seller to take on the obligation to sell you stock at the strike price, if it trades above the strike price at the expiration date.

If for some fundamental or technical reason the stock price appreciates above the strike price, you can exercise your right to buy the stock from the seller at the strike price and reap the benefits of all the capital gains accumulated in the stock. This is good for an investor who believes the stock price will rise substantially and want to have some insurance to lock in profits at a particular price.

Good if you think the stock price will rise.

Where a short position means you are selling, a long position means you are buying. When trading options, you sell to lock in a profit, but take on the obligation to buy or sell the underlying stock. However, when you buy, you pay insurance to lock in a position, and can reap the benefits of buying or selling the underlying stock if the price moves how you anticipated.

Passive Income

Eight hours a day, forty hours a week is the minimum amount of time that most middle class, full time worker spend at their jobs. They trade their time and labor for just enough cash to pay their bills and expenses, maybe have enough for recreational activities with their family, and hopefully save enough for the future. But the honest truth is most people barely have enough cash for their bills. And if a person chooses to engage in recreational activities so they can spend time with their family, they are probably not saving enough for the future.

The hard reality of our current economy and monetary system is that with one stream of income limited by your time and labor, you will never save enough for the future. With the four economic forces working against you, it is impossible to save any substantial amount of cash with one stream of income, which is limited by your time and labor. One of the best ways to generate cash that isn't limited by your time and labor is to create passive income. While that is good advice, it is hard to do if you don't know the most efficient and practical ways to implement this advice.

With all the business opportunities, pyramid schemes and outright scams circulating through the economy, it is difficult to decipher what will actually work. Well let's put it into perspective here. If you have to continuously work to generate income through a so-called business opportunity, and someone else is reaping the benefits of your so-called opportunity, then that so-called opportunity is nothing more than a second job. See our Business Opportunity Fallacy Report. Real passive income should be recurring monthly, or quarterly, from you doing business once. Two of the best methods I have discovered to create passive income, cash that comes in consistently regardless of your time and labor, is through equity and debt. I will explain.

First, I will explain equity. By investing in BDCs, MLPs, REITs, RTs, WDDGs and fundamentally sound Corporations, you can reap the benefits of owning a piece of a strong company that has a track record of not just paying dividends, but also growing them steadily over time. Dividends are monthly, or quarterly payments made to shareholders from the profits earned by a company.

When you invest in a publicly traded company for dividends (or passive income) and not appreciation (i.e. capital gains), you are basically receiving a return on your investment in the form of a yield, or a percentage of your investment per share, per year. Your income will be determined by the market price you purchased your shares at, multiplied by the annual yield, divided by the number of annual payments, multiplied by the number of shares you hold a position in (or own). If you never close your position (or sell your shares) and the dividend is never cancelled, you will continue to receive a steady payment from the company. Obviously if the dividend is increased, decreased or cancelled, your payment will coincide. If you purchase more stock, your dividend will increase according to the number of shares your purchased.

Next, I will explain debt. Unsecured Promissory Notes (or Notes) are debt instruments. A note is a written promise by one party to pay back a loan to another party. Payments are usually made monthly. A note holder is the creditor. The one who promises to pay is the debtor.

The same way banks use debt to get rich you can do the same, and reap the same benefits. By purchasing Unsecured Promissory Notes from a Securities Exchange Commission

(SEC) registered platform, you can effectively play the role of a bank without the time consuming, tedious paperwork and regulations. Notes provide a fairly reliable, fixed cashflow in the form of principal and interest payments made over a predetermined period of time. Unsecured Promissory Notes originate in a bank that issues these notes though an SEC registered platform. By purchasing notes, you are securing passive income for the term of the note.

Unsecured Promissory Notes are usually a good investment when credit is provided to creditworthy individuals.

Because every transaction in a capital gains business structure only pays once, and has to be duplicated repeatedly to maintain a steady cashflow, you cannot accurately forecast operating income (earnings before interest and taxes – EBIT, but after operating expenses) the same way you can with a passive income business structure. In a passive income business structure, business is conducted once and continues to pay a steady cashflow. Here's how it works with our strategy.

Dividends – This is equity income. You purchase 1,000 shares of X-Y-Z stock at $5.00 a share. X-Y-Z stock pays an annual dividend of $1.00 per share which works out to a quarterly dividend of $0.25 per share, or in this case $250. Let's say for example, after your purchase of X-Y-Z stock you have zero cash in your brokerage account and you opt to receive the dividends as payment. Assuming that the dividend isn't lowered, each quarter your cash holdings will increase by $250.

- Payments... Quarter 1, + $250 ($250), Quarter 2, + $250 ($500), Quarter 3, + $250 ($750) Quarter 4, + $250 ($1,000), Quarter 1 (next year) + $250 ($1,250).

As long as X-Y-Z stock is paying a dividend and you are a

shareholder, you will receive that distribution of profits from the company.

Interest – This is debt income. Interest is simply periodic payments made by the borrower, which are in excess of the principal loan amount. When a borrower makes payments, a majority of the payment goes to service the interest in the beginning. As the note is paid off, more of the payment goes to the principal (amount of the loan). Payments are usually amortized, and made monthly in fixed amounts over a fixed period of time.

Theoretically, the less creditworthy the borrower is, the higher the risk of non-payment and default. Conversely, the more creditworthy the borrower is, the less likely they will default on the loan. This is pretty simple.

A fully amortized loan will have principal and interest fixed into each payment to be made by the borrower. Their monthly payments will stay the same, but the amount of the payment that goes towards interest decreases as the loan balance diminishes.

Here's an example of a $1,000 loan at 5% interest over 1 year, fully amortized.

Amortization Table (Monthly)

Loan Amount: **$1,000.00**	Monthly Payment: **$85.61**
Number of Payments: **12.0**	Total Paid: **$1,027.29**
Interest Rate: **5.0%**	Interest Paid: **$27.29**
	Pay-off Date: **Jan 9, 2015**

	Month	Interest	Principal	Balance		Month	Interest	Principal	Balance
1	Jan 2014	$4.17	$81.44	$918.56	7	Jul 2014	$2.11	$83.50	$422.74
2	Feb 2014	$3.83	$81.78	$836.78	8	Aug 2014	$1.76	$83.85	$338.89
3	Mar 2014	$3.49	$82.12	$754.66	9	Sep 2014	$1.41	$84.20	$254.70
4	Apr 2014	$3.14	$82.46	$672.20	10	Oct 2014	$1.06	$84.55	$170.15
5	May 2014	$2.80	$82.81	$589.39	11	Nov 2014	$0.71	$84.90	$85.25
6	Jun 2014	$2.46	$83.15	$506.24	12	Dec 2014	$0.36	$85.25	($0.00)

Compounded Returns

The amount of information available to everyday people that isn't shared, or advertised, is astonishing. There are published government documents that affect our everyday lives we know nothing about. There are policies being made that impact our purchasing power that we know nothing about. And, there are financial opportunities out there that can turn our rags into bags of riches that we know nothing about. But, the fact of the matter is, it is not meant for you to know this information. If you are lucky enough to stumble upon something of value, and figure out how to use it, then kudos to you. However, if you are like the majority of people who don't know, and don't seek out a better way, you will continue to take whatever is given to you by the government, the banks and the corporations.

If you want power and control over your wealth, you must take it. If you want freedom, you must take that as well. One way to achieve power and freedom is through wealth. If you take control of your income and investments and create enough wealth, you should in essence become financially free. There is a simple and effective method in which you can take control of your income and exponentially increase your wealth. This is a published secret that is not advertised, because Wall Street cannot profit from it. They have lobbied government to make it illegal for businesses to advertise this legal investment strategy.

By investing in an 801(k), or what is formally known as a "Dividend Reinvestment Plan", or DRIP, through a publicly traded company's Stock Transfer Agent, you can effectively compound your returns by having your dividends reinvested into the company to purchase more stock. This can compound your returns by up to as much as 4 times your initial investment without ever adding another dime. You can even increase you initial investment by as much as 8 times by purchasing additional stock each month. You can also purchase stock directly from some publicly traded companies via a Direct Stock Purchase Plan (DSPP), through their stock transfer agent.

Compounded returns from stocks are basically when your dividends purchase more shares of a stock, which therefore increases your dividend and allows you to buy more shares of stock. Instead of making gains based solely on your initial investment, you make gains off of the new compounded amount. Probably the best way to see the benefit of your 801(k) is to invest in BDCs, MLPs, REITs, RTs, WDDGs and other fundamentally sound Corporations.

In today's financial system, interest rates are near zero. This means that banks pay almost nothing to borrow money from the Federal Reserve, and in turn, pay you nothing to hold your deposits. Plus, with the September 13, 2012 announcement of QE3 by Federal Reserve Chairman Ben Bernanke, more inflation is set to hit the economy, further devaluing your purchasing power. Savings accounts, treasury bonds, CDs and Money Market Accounts cannot keep up with the level of inflation. A mechanism that can compound your returns and beat inflation is the only way to preserve the value of your dollar denominated holdings.

How does it work? Let's say you purchase 1,000 shares of X-Y-Z stock at $5.00 a share. X-Y-Z pays an annual dividend of $1.00 per share, which works out to a quarterly dividend of $0.25 per share, or in this case $250. Let's say for example you have $50,000 in your brokerage account and you opt to have the dividends reinvested, instead of receiving them as payment. Assuming that the dividend isn't lowered or stopped, each quarter your position in X-Y-Z stock will increase and your dividend will in turn increase, compounding your returns significantly over time as follows (this example also keeps the price the same for the sake of the example):

Reinvestment: Quarter 1, $250 purchases 50 new shares of X-Y-Z stock at $5.00 a share bringing your new position (number of shares owned) to 1,050, and a new dividend of $262.50 to be reinvested. Quarter 2, $262.50 purchases 52.5 new shares of X-Y-Z stock at $5.00 a share bringing your new position to 1,102, and a new dividend of $275.50 to be reinvested. Quarter 3, $275.50 purchases 55.1 new shares of X-Y-Z stock at $5.00 a share bringing your new position to 1,157, and a new dividend of $289.25 to be reinvested. Quarter 4, $289.25 purchases 57.85 new shares of X-Y-Z stock at $5.00 a share bringing your new position to 1,214, and a new dividend of $303.50 to be reinvested.

Not only is this a powerful investment strategy that can significantly increase your wealth, but it also allows you to rest assured that your investment is growing. Banks pay you pennies, at best, in today's economy. Saving cash in a bank and depending on interest from your deposits is basically financial suicide. Cash has to be moving through the economy in order for it to have any true value. Reinvesting your dividends into more shares of stock, keeps your cash circulating. This automatically increases your position in the company, and therefore, increases the value of your holdings.

Hyperinflation Hedge

By converting a portion of your dollar denominated savings into precious metals, namely gold and silver, you can preserve your purchasing power and protect your wealth from inflation, hyperinflation, and any subsequent economic collapse resulting from hyperinflation.

Hyperinflation is the result of excessive, and exponential, increase in the money (i.e. currency) supply. Once hyperinflation hits, prices increase significantly, and the purchasing power of a currency is destroyed (like in the former Soviet Union, Zimbabwe or Argentina). Once the currency is destroyed, the economy eventually collapses. Any wealth denominated in that currency is not destroyed, but rather transferred to those who had the foresight to own precious metals and commodities. Gold and silver are the only commodities that are monetized units of exchange, and are accepted worldwide as a hedge against hyperinflation. Gold and silver in essence preserve purchasing power and any accumulated wealth.

Between Quantitative Easing from the Federal Reserve and bad fiscal policy from the U.S. Government, the U.S. dollar is slowly losing its status as the Reserve Currency of the World. Countries are finding ways to circumvent the Petrodollar, using barter systems of oil for gold, or currency swaps. The U.S. economy is heading towards a hyperinflationary collapse of the currency, which will stem from the Federal Reserve and the U.S. Government trying to avert deflationary events like market crashes and subsequent recessions. Only those who own physical gold and silver will be able to preserve their purchasing power, and have any means of true wealth recognized worldwide in a post petrodollar global economy. Unlike Dollars, Euros, Pounds, Yuan or any other currency, the wealth of precious metals are outside of the control of the banks and any government.

How does it work? Gold and silver are the only monetized precious metals accepted throughout the world. But, in an artificial, centrally manipulated, debt based fiat world, gold and silver have been slept on as being a store of value. Gold and silver have been a store of value for 5,000 years, and will continue to be a store of value for 5,000 more. Here you will see how gold and silver keep up with inflation, and safeguard you current monetary value. For the sake of this example, Gold (Au) will be $1,500 an ounce, and Silver (Ag) will be $30.

Remember, inflation is an increase in the currency supply. Therefore, more cash is chasing finite and limited goods, services and commodities. The value you invest today into precious metals is safe from any hyperinflationary money printing, or quantitative easing by the Federal Reserve, that will devalue the currency, and decrease the purchasing power of your savings.

In our example, inflation is 2% per year.

Year 1	Au = $1,530 Ag = $30.06	Year 2	Au = $1,560.60 Ag = $30.66	Year 3	Au = $1,591.81 Ag = $31.27
Year 4	Au = $1,623.64 Ag = $31.89	Year 5	Au = $1,656.11 Ag = $32.52	Year 6	Au = $1,689.23 Ag = $33.17

Assuming that this chart is correct in the 2 percent annual inflation calculation, Gold (Au) & Silver (Ag) keep up with inflation naturally. The only way they don't keep up with inflation is when the government or central banks artificially suppress prices. Either way, gold and silver continue to be a store of value, because the banks cannot artificially inflate them.

Value Appreciation

By investing in BDCs, MLPs, REITs, RTs, WDDGs and fundamentally sound Corporations that regularly engage in Share Buybacks, you can place yourself in a favorable position to increase the overall value of your shares, and thus increasing your ownership percentage. Share Buybacks decrease the number of outstanding shares a company has, therefore making each remaining share worth more to the shareholder.

Just like when less currency is circulating in the economy, or we enter a deflationary stage and each dollar's value increases, share buybacks cause a stock's value to appreciate sort of in the same way.

By investing in WDDGs, you are inherently investing in the most financially stable, market dominant companies in the world. So, for the most part, your cash is safer being invested in these companies (and some BDCs, MLPs, REITs, RTs, and fundamentally sound corporations) as a shareholder (or unitholder) than it is placed in a bank as an account holder. And they pay you a dividend for being a shareholder. But, what most people don't know is that some of these companies reinvest excess capital to buy back shares of stock instead of increasing dividends. This is good. Why is this good? Well, through a share buyback plan, remaining shareholders are practically receiving a "Stealth Dividend" from the company. This increases the overall value of their shares. Best of all, this stealth dividend is tax-free.

How does it work? Value appreciation is something that you don't specifically have control over. You can either get it through price increase, or through a stealth dividend provided by the company. But, by purchasing shares in companies that engage in what is called a share buyback, you can essentially increase your odds of realizing this value appreciation, in addition to any price increases.

Share Buybacks work like this...

Let's say there are 10,000,000 shares of X-Y-Z stock outstanding at $5.00 per share, which would give X-Y-Z a market cap (number of shares outstanding times the stock price) of $50,000,000. Now, if Earnings per Share (EPS) is $1.00, and Price to Earnings Ratio is 5 (five times earnings) that would mean earnings are $10,000,000. If X-Y-Z initiates and completes a share buyback of 2.5 million shares, that would leave 7.5 million shares outstanding. The new EPS of X-Y-Z would be $1.33, a 33% increase.

How did this happen and how did I get this number? Ten million units (shares) were chasing ten million dollars, hence the one dollar per share. When X-Y-Z bought back 2.5 million units, they took 25% of the units that were chasing the 10 million in earnings out of circulation. This left only 7.5 million units chasing 10 million in earnings. Divide 10 million in earnings by 7.5 million units and you get $1.33; your new earnings per share. The earnings of each share, and therefore the value of each share, were increased by 33% ($0.33 increase, divided by the initial $1.00 EPS). This is powerful. A strategy a publicly traded company can initiate for its shareholders; a stealth, tax free dividend.

Family Banking System

By establishing a participating (dividend paying) Whole Life Insurance Policy with a Paid up Additions Rider (dividends and added cash purchase more death benefit) through a mutual insurance company, you can effectively create your own private family banking system. Not only will you have a lifelong death benefit that will pass to your beneficiaries upon your death tax free, but you will also have your own private, easily accessible compounding savings plan you can use at any time to finance most ordinary large purchases (e.g. a house, a car or an investment property) you would have otherwise used a bank for.

Whether you know this or not, Whole Life Insurance Policies are life insurance policies that are in force for the duration of your life. However, contrary to belief, you only pay the premium for a certain amount of years. These policies accumulate a compounded cash savings, or cash value, that you can borrow from at anytime, for any reason. As long as your premiums are paid on time and the policy doesn't lapse, any loans taken out on the policy are tax-free. And, your cash value continues to compound as if you never took the loan out. Since loans are collateralized by the death benefit, credit checks are not required for loans. In addition to this, the interest you pay back to the policy is basically going back towards compounding the cash value of the policy. A family banking system may be known by other names, but in essence, it is your own personal banking system via whole life insurance.

Instead of paying the banks interest for financing large purchases you would have normally made anyway, you can pay yourself the interest instead through payments you make back to the policy, and save a lot of cash in the process. You are in essence, financing your own purchases, paying yourself the interest (which compounds your cash value) and establishing something that will secure your family financially. And when you borrow from your policy, your cash continues to grow and compound as if you never actually took out a loan. This is one of the best-kept public secrets that banks and corporations use religiously. The poor and middle class have been mislead, miseducated and diverted from the benefits of Whole Life Insurance. If you have ever been told "Buy Term and Invest the Difference", it's because they know if told to do so, the poor and middle class will buy a term life insurance policy. They also know that the odds of having to payout on that policy are slim, so they will pocket every premium the policyholder pays. And, if the policyholder decides they want more life insurance to continue protecting their family, the insurance company can jack up the premium for the new policy.

To add to this horrible advice of "Buy Term and Invest the Difference", not many people know how to actually invest the difference. Most people will either spend the money they received from the closed whole life policy, or they will invest the cash into a status quo investment vehicle, which won't make them rich either. So either way, the poor and middle class are losing money and staying broke. Buy term and invest the difference is status quo advice. How about buy whole life, build your cash value, and then borrow from it to purchase an investment property? Now, that sounds like great advice!

How does it work? With the family banking system, you effectively become your own bank and finance your own large purchases with your own Whole Life Insurance Policy. You pay yourself (and the insurance company) interest on the loan you received from the cash value savings, which in turn compounds your cash value much faster over time. The loan is collateralized by the face value of the policy so there is no recourse, or collections, if you don't pay the loan back; just tax consequences. If the policy lapses or the loan goes unpaid, you must pay taxes on the cash as income. You can substantially reduce the amount of interest and penalties you would have paid, simply by using your private family banking system. This is truly a life benefit more than a death benefit. You can access this cash anytime, for any reason whatsoever, and reap the benefits of paying yourself the interest you would have otherwise given the banks; benefits you reap while you're alive.

Warning: Although this can be an essential tool in your financial planning, whole life insurance can be substantially more expensive depending on various factors like age, face value of the policy and the term of payments. Please see our recommended resource for more information.

UEH Investment Strategy Overview

Incorporation (Forming Legal Entities), Capital Gains (Trading Options), Passive Income (Dividends & Interest Income), Compounded Returns (801k-DRIP), Value Appreciation (Stealth Dividends), Hyperinflation Hedge (Precious Metals) and Family Banking System (Whole Life Insurance).

Forming Legal Entities	Trading Options	Dividends and Interest	801(k) Dividend Reinvestment Plan	Precious Metals	Stealth Dividends	Whole Life Insurance

Industries to Invest In (Stocks & Options)

Oil & Natural Gas Utility	Healthcare	Banking	Personal & Household Products	Real Estate Investment Trusts
Royalties	Biotechnology & Drugs	Insurance	Misc. Financial Services (BDC)	Precious Metals

The 3 UEH Systems

UEH System

I have laid out the investment strategies that make up the Ultimate Economic Hedge, but now I will explain the UEH Systems, and how to make the strategies work best. These are simply recommendations and what we are doing. This is in no way financial, or investment advice. Consult a knowledgeable, qualified professional, or simply do your own due diligence and research, which is recommended.

The 3 Systems

The 3 UEH Systems are comprised of Banking, Trading and Hedging. Each of the 7 strategies works with one of the three systems in their own way. This is our company's recommended method of implementation of the 3 Systems:

Private Banking

Open a whole life insurance policy with a paid up additions rider through a mutual insurance company. Make sure that the policy is a participating policy (one that pays dividends to policy holders). Starting off with a small policy is fine, because the death benefit should increase along with the cash value of the policy. If you happen to reach your max on the policy, you can always open up a second or even third policy.

At some point in the future (5 or more years), borrow from the whole life insurance policy to purchase notes through our recommended resource. Payback the policy at about 9 percent interest with the payments from the notes and reinvest the remaining cash into more notes. This process should continue to build upon itself.

Trading

Use 75 to 80 percent of your world's best business' monthly income to Trade (sell) put options on

BDCs, MLPs, REITs, RTs, WDDGs and fundamentally sound corporations you want to own a position in, and trade (sell) covered call options solely on monthly paying BDCs and MLPs you own a position in.

Buy BDCs, MLPs, REITs, RTs, WDDGs and fundamentally sound Corporations only when they are undervalued.

Undervalued, or cheap, can be considered ten (10) times earnings (net income) or less; fifteen times earnings or less with the most dominant, stable companies. Receive the dividend payments from the monthly dividend paying BDCs, and the MLPs only. Apply a DRIP to all others.

Use what is called a Trailing Stop on your positions to maximize your profits and minimize your losses. This is a form of stop loss that will move with the stock price according to your set parameter (dollar amount or percentage) and trigger a sell order once the price reverses and hits your Trailing Stop trigger. A 25% trailing stop could give you enough of a cushion to have a profitable trade, or cut your losses strategically and effectively. But, however you decide to set your trailing stops is entirely up to you.

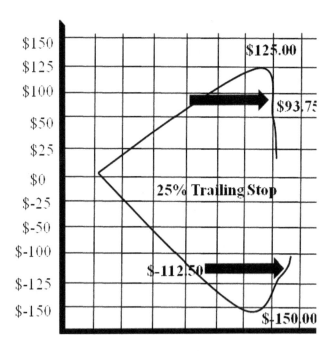

This chart shows how a stop loss called a trailing stop will maximize your profits while limiting your losses. When you are long a stock that means you buy the stock and hold a position in it. When you are short a stock, that means you borrow shares of a stock from your broker to sell the shares.

You go long on a stock if you believe share price will rise, and you short a stock if you believe the share price will fall.

A trailing stop works for both a long position and a short position. In a long or short position, you set either a dollar parameter, or a percentage parameter of when to sell or cover if the share price begins to move against you. The trailing stop will trail the share price as it rises (long) or as it falls (short) and create a new sell (long) or buy (short) trigger price, which will be a percentage or dollar amount of the new high (long) or new low (short) share price. The trailing stop trigger price will only move within the parameter of the new high (long) or new low (short), and will never follow the share price if it begins to move against you. Once the share price hits your new trigger price, a sell order is automatically issued and you will have either made some capital gains or significantly minimized your losses.

There is no premium paid on a trailing stop. You only pay your broker's commission fee for the sell (long) or buy to cover (short) order.

Inflation Hedging

Reinvest the dividends from the remaining non-monthly dividend payers and non-MLPs. This will build upon itself as long as the companies are paying dividends.

Convert 20 to 25 percent of all monthly income to gold and silver bullion you personally own, and can physically hold, in a secure location. This will protect a portion of your savings from the loss of purchasing power suffered through hyperinflation. This also safeguards a portion of your savings from banks and the government, through which their fees, inflation, bailouts, potential bail-ins, taxes, confiscation and other fraudulent schemes would steal your wealth.

You must remain disciplined and stay focused on implementing the system. Don't divert away from the systems. And conduct everything through one, or more, legal entities.

Definitions

World Dominant Dividend Grower (WDDG)

These are blue chip stocks. They are probably the safest investments in the stock market. They pay a quarterly dividend and grow that dividend steadily over the years. WDDGs generally aren't adversely affected by recessions or bad economic conditions, because they are number one, or dominant in their industry.

Master Limited Partnership (MLP)

These are publicly traded limited partnerships. They usually invest in oil, natural gas, infrastructure or commodities and are provided tax exempt status by law as long as they distribute 90% of their earnings to unitholders. Because of government incentives to invest in these structures, there may be favorable tax treatment of income received and expenses of the partnership for unitholders. Please do your own research.

Real Estate Investment Trust (REIT)

These structures can be private, or public companies. They mainly invest in, manage and operate income producing real estate. Once they elect to be taxed as a REIT and they are approved, they are provided tax exempt status by law as long as they distribute 90% of their earnings to unitholders.

Royalty Trust (RT)

These structures can be private or public companies. Royalty Trusts hold the beneficial interest to receive royalties, or a percentage of the sale of oil & gas, or mining resources. Once they elect to be taxed as a royalty trust and they are approved, they are provided tax-exempt status by law as long as they distribute 90% of their earnings to unitholders.

Business Development Company (BDC)

If you ever considered buying stock in a business at the Initial Public Offering (IPO) because you thought it would be a good investment, you are not alone. Many people believe buying stock in a newly publicly traded company at an IPO is a good investment, because the stock can only go higher from there. But, as those investors who purchased Facebook at its May 18, 2012 IPO soon realized, IPOs are not always the best investment. In fact, unless you actually bought your share at the open for $42 per share and immediately sold them at the high of $45 before the stock plummeted to a low of $38, you lost money. And, it would have taken you over a year to recuperate any of those losses.

The honest truth is that all of the big money in Facebook was made well before the IPO. Most investors who got in on the IPO got slaughtered. Some may call Facebook a pump and dump scheme, but the fact is that the company was worth more private than it was at its IPO. How so? Well, there are companies that provide funding, management and usually take an equity stake in up and coming companies with a proven or safe business model. These companies are called BDCs, or Business Development Companies.

BDCs are a back door into a private stock market that is accessible by only 6 percent of investors. Only 6 percent of investors are allowed to access this backdoor market due to their accredited high net worth and insider connections to these companies. The other 94 percent are left out. This backdoor market is where the real money in companies like Facebook and Groupon are made. BDCs get access to companies like these well before they go public, and some that actually never go public.

BDCs provide financing for small cap, and middle market companies, provide management and consultation services, and receive either equity in the company, or interest payments. Since BDCs invest in companies with proven products and services, or show solid growth potential, there is little risk associated with a BDC's investments.

BDCs are not taxed at the federal level as long as they distribute 90% of their capital gains, interest and other investment income to their shareholders. And, most BDCs pay high yields, with some as high as 14%. Where most BDCs pay quarterly dividends, there are a select few that actually pay monthly dividends to their shareholders.

Unspoken of Assets

MLPs, REITs, RTs and BDCs are unspoken of asset classes of stock, not advertised to the general public, just like the 801(k) plan, or any investment that would give the middle class person an advantage to achieve wealth. WDDGs are more widely advertised, but are not singled out for the benefits I have mentioned here. They are touted more for their brand recognition and high trading volume.

Community Corporation

Citizens United

You may or may not know this, but in 2010, the U.S. Supreme Court reversed a decision by the United States District Court for the District of Columbia in Citizens United v. Federal Election Commission , 558 U.S. 310 (2010) stating the First Amendment prohibited the government from restricting independent political expenditures by corporations and unions. This case came about when Citizens United wanted to air a film criticizing Hilary Clinton before the 2008 Democratic primaries. It would have aired within 30 days of the primaries, which would have been a violation of the Bipartisan Campaign Reform Act (BCRA). The BCRA prohibits unions, corporations and not-for-profit organizations from broadcasting electioneering communications within 60 days of a general election or 30 days of a primary election. The Supreme Court held that BRCA §203 violates the free speech clause of the First Amendment to the United States Constitution.

What does this have to do with anything? Well, the fact that this ruling was made in favor of a corporation is basically saying that corporations have the same First Amendment right as people, and their political spending is a form of freedom of speech. Now, although Citizens United seemingly is a corporation with a noble goal centered around "restoring government to citizens' control", this decision opened the flood gates for huge corporations, that don't have the American citizens' best interest, or our nation's sovereignty at heart, to use their huge cash reserves to create political advertisements in favor of a candidate who they have ties with.

This may seem like a scary direction, and seemingly puts the individual citizen at a disadvantage. Well, it is a scary direction and it does put the individual citizen at a disadvantage. But, if you take a play out of the book of Corporations, and get a little savvy, you can effectively give yourself the same advantage as a huge corporate conglomerate or an international bank. How? Look at this word... "Citizens United". This concept of citizens uniting under a corporate entity in the name of freedom, or any cause, isn't new, but it may be new to you. And here is how you can apply it to your life.

Community Corporation

You probably never thought of forming a corporation. You may have considered a corporation as some huge, mystical entity that controls various resources and sells products and services that we cannot live without. You may think that owning a corporation requires millions and millions of dollars, and ordinary people don't have a shot at being in a position of control in a huge corporation. Well, allow me to tell you with confidence that you are absolutely dead wrong. A corporation is nothing more than an official legal entity created under something called "Articles of Incorporation" (or Articles of Organization for LLCs and LPs) filed with the Secretary of State, which has a separate identity from its owners (shareholders). That's it.

You could form what I like to refer to as a "Community Corporation". What is a community corporation and what would a community corporation do, you ask? First, a community corporation is a regular corporation formed by you and other citizens within your local community. Every financially contributing citizen can be a shareholder. Price per share can be established however the shareholders see fit. And second, a community corporation could invest its cash into income producing assets (e.g. dividend yielding stocks, real estate or local businesses) and utilize its profits to beautify the community, create local community programs, advocate for local businesses and lobby government for neighborhood and citywide (or countywide) improvements.

The community corporation could even publish newsletters and sell subscriptions locally.

Any group of people elected by the shareholders can be the Board of Directors, which is the governing body that makes the decisions on policies, procedures and appointment of Officers (or Executive Managers). Anyone can be elected as the Chairman of the Board. The Board can appoint anyone as Chief Executive Officer, President, Chief Financial Officer, Vice President and Secretary. Once established, your community corporation can effectively serve the same purpose as these huge multi-million dollar and billion dollar corporations, and that is to further the interest of its shareholders. Remember, there is strength in numbers.

Begging for a Quarter

People that work in the private sector, and some applicable public sector jobs, often complain that they work many long hours, but don't get the raise they feel they are "owed".

The fact of the matter is that businesses and government agencies that hire people do not owe their employees a penny more than what they agreed to pay them when they hired them.

Imagine you hired a contractor to fix three rooms in your house for $500 per room and they agree to that wage. Then towards the end of the second room, they all of a sudden want to be paid $750 because they feel entitled to more compensation for the work they've already done. So now, they expect you to find another $250 to pay them, when they already agreed to work for $500 per room.

Most people not only look for the false security of a job, but also feel entitled to extra just because they work 40 hours a week, trading their time and labor for cash. They usually look for extra handouts for their time and labor, even though they already agreed to a set amount. Most people never ask themselves "how can I make my current cash and income work for me?"

Well the hard, honest truth is that if the wage slaves, a.k.a. the employees, actually took the time to educate themselves and invested in the very companies or industries they work countless hours for, not only would the economy naturally improve from the increased investments by the working class, and the new cash flow into these companies, but on the right investment, these employees would earn a passive income from cash they would have otherwise spent frivolously on depreciating junk.

If these employees slowly increased their position in these companies or industries over time, they would either build up a small nest egg of cash through dividends, eventually surpassing their full time 40 hour per week income, or they would compound their returns significantly higher over time through the 801(k) Plan. All this without any extra handouts or burdens placed on the business they work for. Best of all, they would receive payments from that business in two ways; first through earned income from wages paid to them for doing their job, and second, through passive income from dividends (distribution of profits) for being a shareholder.

If you are employed by Walmart and work 40 hours a week at a rate of $10.00 per hour, chances are you won't get rich, or make much more than that for the rest of the time you work there. Most employees will work countless hours in hopes they get a quarter raise, or even just a ten cents from management. Breaking your back in hopes for a quarter is sad, but that's the only thing that most people know.

But, for those smart, ambitious employees who don't want to wait for Walmart (or any other company) to give them a quarter, but instead want to legally extract dollars from the company they work for, they will look to own a piece of the company. So now, by owning a piece of the company, they have a vested financial interest in seeing this business succeed and grow. And, when they get their first dividend check, they will know the proud feeling of being a shareholder.

End of Freedom

Economic Problems

A majority of our country's economic problems could easily be eliminated if this country (i.e. government and citizens) took the following actions:

Government:

1. Stop borrowing currency from the Federal Reserve. The printing and supplying of our nation's currency

should be the sole responsibility of the United States Treasury. Determining the value of that currency and how it is spent should be the sole responsibility of our United States Congress. No private institution (yes, private with shareholders) should have the responsibility, let alone the monopoly to control the money supply and the value thereof.

2. Impose and enforce regulations on financial institutions. Regulations like the Dodd-Frank Act passed by President Obama on July 21, 2010 have done little to protect people from the fraudulent financial system. When MF Global stole the money of account holders like Gerald Celente, publisher of the Trends Journal, and others who entrusted their investment fund to them, prosecutions should have been lining up. But, CEO and former New Jersey Governor Jon Corzine, who apparently signed off on money transfers from customer accounts, has yet to see, or even have charges filed, against him.

3. Stop funding an empire. All empires eventually fall. It happened to the Romans, The Ottomans, The Persians, The Mongols and even the great British Empire. Funding an empire is costly in more ways than one. U.S. military presence in sovereign countries is not only a sign of arrogance, but also a blatant disregard for their sovereignty. We have plenty of territory without having military bases in other countries.

4. Eliminate the federal, state and local income tax. Every citizen and business under the jurisdiction of the United State should not be required to pay a tax on their income. Money paid to the government by individuals in the form of taxes could be spent into the

economy and businesses could reinvest that money into production and employment.

5. Eliminate taxes on utilities. Only manufactured goods sold, foreign imports, alcohol and tobacco should be taxed. Utilities like internet (and similar digital services), electricity, water and gas should not be taxed. Yet again, the more money people have in their pockets, the more money will be spent into the economy. That will equal more tax revenue from goods, imports, alcohol and tobacco.

6. Reduce government size. There is one executive department, along with its subordinate agencies, that duplicates the functions of a number of other departments. That department is the Department of Homeland Security. The Department of Homeland Security has 8 child agencies under it. Five of those eight agencies perform duplicate functions of other U.S. Departments and agencies, which is totally unnecessary. Get rid of the DHS.

7. Stop government subsidies of education. Student loan debt is over $1,000,000,000,000 (that's trillion) and growing. With the economy in a continuous recession (and projected to get worse by 2016), the actual unemployment rate higher than official numbers and our national debt accumulating, future college graduates have a pretty bleak world to come into. Everyone and anyone can go to college and get a bachelor's, Master's or doctoral degree. The government guarantees most of these loans. So, our friends the banks (not Phil, Vivian, Hilary, Carlton and Ashley) will lend cash to anyone who fills out a loan application, because there is no risk. If anyone can get a degree, where

is the prestige? There is none. Then, when everyone graduates and looks for employment, there is little supply of jobs available. The graduating class from 4 years ago took all the jobs. Allow people's academics to determine who goes to college and stop subsidizing education.

8. Decommission and disband the Federal Reserve. The Federal Reserve has not lived up to its duel mandate of stable prices and high employment since its inception in 1913. Plus, the Federal Reserve lends our government its own money at interest automatically putting our government into debt (and thus, the people). And, the Federal Reserve is responsible for supervising the banking system which has cause financial distress not only to individual citizens, but also our entire country. Eliminate the Federal Reserve.

9. Adhere to the U.S. Constitution. If we go back to the mindset that made this country great and prosperous, maybe we could get back on track to being a wealthy country instead of a nation deep in debt. Apply the following: 1. Stop passing laws that violate civil liberties and constitutional rights, 2. Create sound money using gold and silver, and not privately controlled fiat debt money, 3. Let the U.S. Treasury manage our country's money and the U.S. Congress determine its use and allocation, 4. Only create federal regulations, which stop state level oppression and violations of constitutional rights, 5. Make Government's top 5 priorities safety within our boarders, employment for all U.S. residents, nationwide economic stability, Infrastructure upgrades and free job training for the poor and homeless. If a star athlete starts to lose his or

her edge, a good coach will always tell them practice the basics to refine their skills. Let's Get Back To The Basics.

10. Stop the Damn Handouts. Unemployment insurance is necessary for someone who has lost their job and needs assistance to get back on their feet. But, all of these other social programs like welfare, social security, government pensions, Medicare and others like them only make people dependent on the government. Dependency only leads to laziness, lack of motivation and a sense of entitlement after a while. These people drain government revenue without contributing to the economy. People should be forced (not by government, but by having no other means) to privately invest for retirement, purchase an insurance plan to cover medical, dental and eyes, and maintaining their financial security. You may say, well not everyone knows how to do that. True! But, there is an abundance of information, classes and experts that can teach people money management techniques, investment techniques and financial literacy. So, there is no excuse.

Citizens:

1. Get a Financial Education. One of this country's main problems is the lack of financial education each citizen has. Financial education is not taught in high school or college because the financial elite does not want the middle class to know (and understand) what they know. Invest in your own financial education. Learn about business, investing, our financial and monetary systems and factors that affect our economy.

The same type of information Too Broke to 2 Billion, LLC provides in our book It's Not Your Fault! and website GuidanceProgram.net.

2. Know the U.S. Constitution. Each citizen's individual ignorance of our country's constitution is one of the main reasons for our government expanding in size, infringing upon our civil liberties, violating our constitutional rights and engaging in illegal wars. We briefly learn about the Constitution in high school, but never actually study it. Before all of our rights and liberties are stripped from us by the financial elite and our government, we all must learn and understand the U.S. Constitution. That is the only thing that keeps us from becoming slaves and sheep to our government and monetary system.

3. Don't believe everything you hear on the news. The mainstream media is controlled, and owned, by the same financial elite that control our financial and monetary systems, place whole nations in debt, finance wars and play with credit derivatives (transfer of risk). Do your own research when you hear something on the news. There is a lot of alternative media on the internet, satellite radio and internet radio that reports the real story. One good source of non-corporate media is Russia Today. Don't let the name fool you. Their news shows such as Breaking the Set and Keiser Report provides a comprehensive platform for financial education and information on world economics. You can find Russia Today on both YouTube and their website RT.com.

4. Be open to education, self-improvement and bettering your situation. Education, self-improvement and

bettering your situation all involve a little risk and stepping outside of your comfort zone. You need to accept the risk and take ownership over bettering your situation. Ignorant and close-minded people can never excel in life, or be anything more than what they currently are. Become a master of your environment and not a slave to your fears.

5. Learn how to determine the difference between an isolated act of crime and an apparent staged event concocted to implement laws to take away your economic freedom, constitutional rights and civil liberties. This skill will open your eyes to possible deception and dissuade you from cosigning (through your support) implementation of bills that gives the government more control over your life. No act of terrorism calls for government to strip the liberties of its citizens. That is entirely government's excuse to exercise more totalitarian control over all resources (natural and human).

Both the government and Citizens lists entail a lot of restructuring and adjustment. But, the willingness to change and strive for better is the first step. Accepting the status quo and allowing current situations to remain as they are is only going to bring this country down even further into the pits of hell. We have become a slave to our monetary system, instead of our monetary system serving us like it once did. People are like brainless zombies moving around with no purpose, being lead and controlled like sheep on a farm. Our labor (which we are taxed on the fruits of) and faith in our currency, is the only thing keeping this country from heading into an economic collapse. But, that faith is slowly dwindling and coming to an end. Open your eyes and see the truth before it is too late.

New World Order Mark of the Beast

Most people have heard about the Bible prophesized, "Mark of the Beast" where you cannot purchase goods and services, or travel, without an identifying stamp affixed to your body. This type of system, where your very existence as a citizen depends on your daily interaction with this identifying mark, strips people of their individuality and economic freedoms. Understanding the level of economic slavery and the surrendering-of-privacy requirements associated with this system, will help you realize the sadistic mindset of those who would seek to implement it.

You need to understand that this type of technology currently exists, and how it will be used will ultimately abolish your civil liberties and constitutional rights. Technology is a beautiful thing when used benevolently for the benefit of mankind and nature. However, when technology is used for sinister and malevolent purposes, it ultimately will destroy the very society it was supposed to serve. Drawing the line as to how you decide to use technology in your life will ultimately dictate the level of influence it will have over you later. Invasive and intrusive technology cannot play a role in our everyday lives. When it does, it becomes a controlling factor and gains power from its perceived relevance.

Have you ever heard of the New World Order? A lot of people have, but most people are not aware of what the New World Order is exactly. The New World Order refers to what the financial elite (and former President George H.W. Bush) call a one world government. This is where all political and economic power is concentrated under the control of one global state or organization. Although it's on a smaller scale, the European Union and proposed African Union are working towards this very concept; centralized economic policies which eliminate the sovereignty of each nation.

Why is this bad? Well, centralized economic power, which eliminates the sovereignty of a nation ultimately, becomes the ruler of that nation. He who controls the money of a nation has absolute power. A quote by Mayer Amschel Rothschild, of the Rothschild Family Banking Dynasty, goes "Give me control of a nation's money supply, and I care not who makes its laws". This statement illustrates the understanding Rothschild had that control of money allows control of not just people, but also nations. Centralized control of money puts the wealth of the nation in the hands of a few, and eliminates any economic freedoms one may have under a free economy.

What is the point of all this? Well, in the spirit of the "Mark of the Beast" prophecy, there is technology that is capable of, and created to, erase your freedom. I am going to highlight three technologies that currently exist which provide the government and the financial elite the capabilities to implement the Mark of the Beast, or their 666 Stamp, on you at any given moment. You will see prophecy flash right before your eyes. If you don't believe in the Bible, then understand this technology poses a threat to your civil liberties and constitutional rights. Once financial institutions and government implement this technology, you will become a slave to a system that could have been avoided.

Consolidation of Information

The first technology provides the capacity to store infinite amounts of data on anything imaginable throughout the world. What is the name of this technology? Well, the term cloud computing came from the creation of this technology. In the same way Alternating Current (AC) Electricity replaced Direct Current (DC) Electricity and revolutionized how electricity was provided, this technology will effectively eliminate the use of PC storage and memory drives by use of Cloud Computing. What I'm referring to is Data Centers.

Data Centers are huge warehouse like buildings that are created for the sole purpose of storing huge amounts of data. Think about it, if we can purchase a personal two terabyte external hard drive, which can hold a seemingly endless amount of files, then imagine what a warehouse full of those two terabyte hard drives can do. Now imagine one of those warehouses in every major city in the United States. Well, most large corporations have their own data centers, which hold information about their customers, business operations and financials. This type of technology is used by financial institutions and government to store information on us every day. They keep track of our activities, our habits and our transactions.

Human Tracking

The second technology allows for the wireless and contactless transfer of information about a subject from an affixed personally identifying tag, which uses radio frequency to transmit that information. This type of technology can identifying and track merchandise, cattle or cargo anywhere in the world. Sort of like a bar code for a product, this technology marks an item with its own personal identification tag. But, unlike a bar code, this technology isn't limited by line of sight requirements to read information. This amazing technology is called Radio Frequency Identification, or RFID.

RFID tags or chips can be place on, or implanted into, a subject. The problem with this is if RFID become the way in which people pay for food and conduct transactions, we will become slaves to our RFID. Whoever controls what your RFID reads, or doesn't read, inherently controls you. For example, if you do not like a policy and you wish to protest or speak against it, but you need your RFID to purchase food or conduct transactions, the RFID controllers can essentially deactivate your chip or tag to punish you. You will be rendered helpless. As a result of this, the RFID becomes the new money and the RFID controllers become the new Federal Reserve. We could eventually see a new monetary system in the form of the "RFID Credit System".

Cashless Society

The third technology enables contactless exchange of data between two wireless or mobile devices. This technology is used in E-Z Pass, Mobile Phones, iPads and other wireless devices. It is basically built upon RFID technology and will soon replace credit cards, rendering them obsolete. Rendering an innovation like the credit card obsolete is a huge feat. This technology has to have a competitive advantage. Disrupting the credit card industry to the point to where the physical card becomes obsolete means a revolution in how we conduct transactions. What am I referring to?

Near Field Communication (NFC) technology is a communication standard between smartphones, and other wireless devices. It allows them to establish radio communication by either touching, or being in close proximity of each other. This type of technology can make our lives so much more efficient. It would eliminate the need for cash and credit cards all together. No more clunky wallets, cards and dollar bills. But, this is exactly the type of technology that works into the plans of the financial elite and one world government. This is the ingredient needed to phase out paper money and only have digital money. Just like the fiat currency the Federal Reserve irresponsibly prints, disproportionate to the production of real goods and services, digital money can easily be manipulated. But, in this case, it is done completely with the stroke of a key. No physical money ever comes into existence.

Loss of Liberty

If the world become the victim of a new monetary system which eliminates physical money and forces each citizen to wear a personally identifying tag, which not only transmits information about them, but also requires them to conduct all transactions through that tag, all civil liberties, constitutional rights and national sovereignty will effectively be destroyed. We will be plugged into a hellish global nightmare of information collection and sharing. Sort of like the Matrix, you will be just another expendable element in the system once you have no use. The only difference here will be, you will be awake and know it.

Do Not Give Up Your Civil Liberties and Constitutional Rights for:

- National Security
- Alleged Terrorist Threats
- Personal Convenience
- Government Regulations
- Media Propaganda
- Or anything else that infringes on your civil liberties and constitutional rights

On March 16, 2012, while everyone was out preparing to celebrate (or not celebrate) St. Patrick's Day, our "Yes We Can" fake pillar of hope president, Barack Obama signed a bill into law that had oppressive overtones and "Violation of Constitutional Rights" written all over it called the National Defense Resource Preparedness Order. The National Defense Resource Preparedness Order is basically a step towards martial law in our country. Under this executive order, absolute authority is bestowed upon the various secretaries through the president. For example:

1. Secretary of Defense – now has power over all water resources.
2. Secretary of Commerce – now has power over all material services and facilities (including construction materials)
3. Secretary of Transportation – now has power over all forms of civilian transportation.
4. Secretary of Labor – now has power over all labor resources (U.S. Citizens) and can allocate such resources as deemed necessary.

This order does not require a national emergency, or a threat to national safety to be enacted. They don't need a specific reason to justify implementing such measures. They can simply say, "It's for national defense, now deal with it". Understand that you can effectively be ordered to work anywhere for the purpose of national defense. This bill was silently and thoughtfully passed without the knowledge of the people.

The National Defense Resource Preparedness Order was an extension of the National Defense Authorization Act

(NDAA), which allows the President to indefinitely detain any American citizen who is suspected of being a terrorist. Yes, "any American Citizen" who is even "Suspected" of being a terrorist. You don't have to be convicted, or even indicted to be detained. If you are said to be a terrorist, they can detain you until their itch to hold you is scratch. The funny thing is, you will probably end up in the one place that President Obama stated, and promised, he would close down; and that is Guantanamo Bay, Cuba. Good luck ever seeing freedom after you end up there.

The government is supposed to serve and protect the citizens of the United States, and be for the people, and by the people. The government is not supposed to dictate to, or manipulate the people. We are supposed to live in a free society, but that is slowly becoming a concept of fiction. Don't surrender your freedom. Get educated and resist any infringements upon personal freedom, and all forms of tyranny.

Resources

For a list of alternative media resources, economic and government related information, gold and silver information, the U.S. Constitution in its entirety and access to our It's Not Your Fault! Guidance Program, visit our website:
guidanceprogram.net

Follow us on Twitter:
@TBT2B @GuidanceProgram @MTLeader

Financial & Business Resources
Legal Zoom (Incorporation) – http://legalzoom.com
TD Ameritrade (Brokerage) – http://tdameritrade.com
Prosper (Note Trading Platform) – http://prosper.com
Paradigm Life (Whole Life Insurance) –
http://paradigmlife.net
PayPal (Online Merchant Account) – http://paypal.com
Stock Transfer Agents (DRIP & DSPP):
American Stock Transfer & Trust – http://amstock.com
Computershare – http://computershare.com
Wells Fargo Shareowner Online –
http://shareowneronline.com
CST Trust Company – http://canstockta.com
Rich Dad, Poor Dad (Rich Dad Book) –
http://store.richdad.com
Conspiracy of the Rich (Rich Dad Book) –
http://store.richdad.com

Unless otherwise expressed, we do not receive any compensation for recommending any of the aforementioned financial or business resource.

Our It's Not Your Fault "Guidance Program" consists of 1 year of unlimited email correspondence with the author, a 12-month financial statement spreadsheet created by the author you can use for daily accounting, a put-call transaction forecast spreadsheet you can use to predict profits, losses or discounts on trades and a private instructional video, which explains the 7 Ultimate Economic Hedge strategies. Access to our Guidance Program is available exclusively at:
GuidanceProgram.net

NOTES

NOTES